Executive Assistant and Managerial Handbook

The Definitive Executive Assistant and Managerial Handbook

A professional guide to leadership for all PAs, Senior Secretaries, Office Managers and Executive Assistants

Sue France

KoganPage

LONDON PHILADELPHIA NEW DELHI

Publisher's note

Every possible effort has been made to ensure that the information contained in this book is accurate at the time of going to press, and the publishers and author cannot accept responsibility for any errors or omissions, however caused. No responsibility for loss or damage occasioned to any person acting, or refraining from action, as a result of the material in this publication can be accepted by the editor, the publisher or the author.

First published in Great Britain and the United States in 2012 by Kogan Page Limited

120 Pentonville Road
London N1 9JN
United Kingdom
www.koganpage.com

1518 Walnut Street, Suite 1100
Philadelphia PA 19102
USA

4737/23 Ansari Road
Daryaganj
New Delhi 110002
India

© Sue France, 2012

The right of Sue France to be identified as the author of this work has been asserted by her in accordance with the Copyright, Designs and Patents Act 1988.

ISBN   978 0 7494 6582 7
E-ISBN   978 0 7494 6583 4

British Library Cataloguing-in-Publication Data

A CIP record for this book is available from the British Library.

Library of Congress Cataloging-in-Publication Data

France, Sue.
  The definitive executive assistant and managerial handbook : a professional guide to leadership for all PAs, senior secretaries, office managers and executive assistants / Sue France.
    p. cm.
    ISBN 978-0-7494-6582-7 – ISBN 978-0-7494-6583-4   1. Administrative assistants–Handbooks, manuals, etc.   2. Secretaries–Handbooks, manuals, etc.   3. Office management–Handbooks, manuals, etc.   4. Office practice–Handbooks, manuals, etc.   I. Title.
    HF5547.5.F688 2013
    651.3–dc23
                                                                                        2012025895

Typeset by Graphicraft Limited, Hong Kong
Print production managed by Jellyfish
Printed and bound by CPI Group (UK) Ltd, Croydon, CR0 4YY

Dedication

This book is dedicated to my two daughters without whom my life would not be so fulfilled and joyous. My eldest daughter, Sara Reading (née Hoodfar), and my youngest daughter, Samantha Higgins, who continue to love, support and encourage me in everything I do.

I also dedicate this book to Sara's precious daughter – my granddaughter, as it's a wonderful and overwhelming feeling to have the opportunity to be a proud grandmother to Bella, who always makes me smile. She melts my heart and brings joy and laughter to us all. I simply feel blessed to have such a wonderful family.

I also dedicate this book to each and every proactive assistant around the world for all the hard work you do with such passion and enthusiasm. Thank you for buying this book, which I hope gives you wisdom and knowledge and helps motivate and encourage you to keep on learning and aiming high.

CONTENTS

09   The art and science of effective negotiation   169

10   Change management: how can you help?   194

Resources

FOREWORD

Lucy Brazier, CEO, Marcham Publishing, Publishers of Executive Secretary and *The VA Magazine*

A fifth of the world's working population works in administrative roles. Often undervalued and usually misunderstood, administrative professionals play key roles in their companies, supporting their executives to allow them to be the best that they can be.

Whether you are an Office Junior at entry level – or an Administrative Director looking after huge teams of administrative professionals – with the onslaught of the recession four years ago, the role has never been so important to a company's growth.

With the collapse of Lehman Brothers in 2008, the subsequent recession has forced the biggest shift in the role of the administrative professional since the invention of the internet and the biggest opportunity.

It's an exciting time for the market.

Assistants are being asked to take on roles that middle management traditionally used to do, because so many of them have been made redundant. The role is evolving at lightning speed. Those not willing to embrace the changes and hoping to keep their heads below the parapet will quickly become expendable.

If you don't like change, you are going to like irrelevance even less.
(General Eric Shinseki)

The post-recession business environment for administrative professionals requires a whole new way of thinking and a new level of understanding about the challenges of leadership and management in the corporate world.

No longer the stereotypical typist, message taker, gatekeeper and diary manager, the role has become so diverse and creative that the challenge has become how to define and regulate it across the marketplace to provide structure, career progression and training – because suddenly assistants at all levels are managing not only their executives but also projects and often people too. A strategic partner rather than just a support mechanism, the modern Assistant is a crucial part of any business.

Just as in her first book, *The Definitive Personal Assistant and Secretarial Handbook*, Sue France wholly understands the need for an in-depth practical and inspirational guide to the skill sets needed by an Administrative Assistant. This new companion, *The Definitive Executive Assistant and Managerial Handbook* takes this one step further, looking at the leadership and management skills that are now a necessity. The advice in this book is key to empowering the Assistant – allowing them to assert their leadership qualities within this constantly changing new role in order to progress in their careers.

Sue France is uniquely positioned to write this book. With over 30 years of experience as a top level assistant, she is in now in such demand as a trainer that she is rarely out of the classroom. I would suspect that in the last two years, Sue has probably met more Assistants in more countries than any other trainer in the world. She has listened to their stories and discovered at first-hand how the role is developing and what their issues and needs are.

Sue encompasses all that she writes about in this new book. A true leader – innovative and inspirational, you couldn't ask for a better role model to offer advice on these qualities and skills and what they will mean to you and your career.

The new-world Assistant understands the need to be constantly evolving, stretching their abilities, facing challenges and leading the way. Suddenly, Assistants are the glue that holds a business together. As an Assistant is often the only one to have the full picture as a connector between people or departments, they are in a unique position to use their knowledge and skills to help the business and its employees to make informed decisions – to lead from the front.

When this recession shakes down and we finally come out at the other end, the role of the Assistant will have been redefined beyond recognition to encompass more responsibility and with it the respect that the profession deserves and has needed for so long. The wheat is rapidly being separated from the chaff. It's up to you which category you end up in.

ABOUT THE AUTHOR
Sue France, FCIPD, INLPTA

After working in the secretarial field for over 30 years, Sue France set up her own training business for assistants in November 2009, which has taken her all over the world. Whilst working for a training and development company, Persuasion, in 2006, she won the prestigious title of 'The Times Crème/DHL PA of the Year.' Sue was also a finalist in the Smart European PA of the Year 2007 and since then she has been the judge of several PA of the Year awards, including the UK Times Crème/Hays PA of the year 2007.

Sue is an internationally renowned professional motivational speaker, coach and trainer and the author of the worldwide best-selling book *The Definitive Personal Assistant & Secretarial Handbook* – 2nd edition.

Sue is a certified Neuro-Linguistic Programming (NLP) practitioner and a qualified learning and development practitioner, as well as a fellow of the Chartered Institute of Personnel and Development and an associate trainer for Reed Learning UK. In 2012 she was certified as a TetraMap® behavioural profiling facilitator. Sue is on the editorial board of the global magazine for secretaries, *Executive Secretary*, and regularly writes articles for this magazine and other publications.

Her career began as a shorthand typist/word-processing operator, becoming a senior secretary, team supervisor, events manager and personal assistant to the head of a global leading accounting firm. Whilst working full time, Sue attended university as a mature student two nights a week for three years and gained a postgraduate diploma in human resource management. She then became the UK training manager responsible for 600 secretaries in the UK.

From 2002 to 2009 Sue worked for Bill Docherty of Persuasion, an international motivational speaker, as his PA, global marketing, training and events manager, trainer/coach for assistants as well as being Bill's co-presenter at PA conferences worldwide. She is now the UK National Chairman for European Management Assistants (EUMA), a voluntary secretarial networking organization in 26 countries that promotes learning and self-development as well as global networking with like-minded assistants.

Sue has also been involved in raising money for children's charities by participating in sponsored walks on the Great Wall of China, the Inca Trail in Peru, Mount Etna and the Grand Canyon amongst others. Sue is the proud mother of Samantha and Sara and is now the proud and doting grandmother of Bella.

How to contact the author: I would be delighted to hear from you and I am happy to travel anywhere in the world to facilitate workshops and speak at conferences. You can contact me for one-to-one coaching in the UK and telephone coaching or Skype coaching around the world. My e-mail address is **sue@suefrance.com** and you can also contact me via my website at **www.suefrance.com** or via LinkedIn: **http://uk.linkedin.com/in/suefrance**, Facebook: **https://www.facebook.com/SueFranceTraining** or you can follow me on **Twitter @suefrance**.

ACKNOWLEDGEMENTS

I would like to acknowledge my two wonderful and loving daughters for their unconditional support and love: Sara Hoodfar and Samantha Higgins who understand me and what I do and enable me to write my books and encourage me to continue to conduct my workshops worldwide.

I would like to give a huge thank you to every one of you who have bought my first book and my 2nd edition of *The Definitive Personal Assistant & Secretarial Handbook* and/or this book.

I would also like to thank all those who have hired me to speak at conferences and workshops around the world. I have thoroughly enjoyed meeting everyone and having the opportunity to work in so many different cultures and with so many different personalities. The interaction of all assistants has been amazing and also useful as I continually learn and grow with the knowledge I gain from you.

I would also like to thank and show my appreciation to the following organizations and people for their help with input into this book:

First of all my publisher, Kogan Page and in particular my editor – Liz Barlow – who has been a tremendous help with advice and helping me to achieve my goals and my deadlines.

Belbin.com 2012 for allowing me to reproduce Belbin® Team Roles. For more information on Belbin® please see their website: **www.belbin.com**.

I would also like to acknowledge my thanks to all my colleagues in European Management Assistants as this organization is made up of assistants who continue to work tirelessly as volunteers to network and learn with like-minded people. I especially thank the European executive team and the UK team who work closely with me with such passion and enthusiasm, and in particular Adam Fidler, the UK Public Relations Officer, and Angela Mistry, the UK National Treasurer. I would also like to thank all the Regional EUMA UK Chairmen who regularly organize training events where we all continue to learn and network as all this contributes to my personal learning and enhances my knowledge that I can pass on to you.

Sharon Severn, Sec/PA to Bob Stoddart, Rolls-Royce plc for sharing her team's Mission Statement.

Julie French, Director of Academy of High Achievers Ltd and a Certified Trainer in 'Everything DiSC'. If you would like more information on DiSC® Julie would love to hear from you. Her e-mail address is **jfrench@aha-success.com** and website is **www.aha-success.com**.

Catherine Thomas, PA for the Director of Shared Services Partnership, NHS Wales, who has successfully organized an internal PA network.

Kevin Dennison INLPTA, an accredited NLP trainer and NLP Master Practitioner who trained and certified me as an NLP practitioner.

Ann Clews, the UK TetraMap® Master Teacher for certifying me as a TetraMap® facilitator.

Yoshimi and Jon Brett, founders of TetraMap®, for allowing me to reproduce information on TetraMap® behavioural styles. If you would like to know more about the TetraMap® behavioural profiling workshops for assistants please contact Sue France at **sue@suefrance.com** or see **www.tetramap.com**.

Introduction

As a leader, or someone who wants to instil leadership qualities into their everyday lives, you will find *The Definitive Executive Assistant and Managerial Handbook* your most knowledgeable and motivating friend; it will act as a reference book full of insights, tips, tools, advice and earned wisdom for you to dip into and out of when looking for inspiration, support and answers. You will find insights and top tips learned from years of experience, research and from my personal learning.

This book builds on learning from the best-selling book *The Definitive Personal Assistant & Secretarial Handbook*, 2nd edition, published in August 2012. The two books complement each other and can be bought as a set to be used as your friend, advisor and motivator enabling you to be the most effective and efficient assistant and leader, helping you to progress in your career. This book assumes that you are already proficient in communicating and building relationships as well as in technical areas and computer programs such as Word, Excel, Outlook/diary, contact databases and PowerPoint, and are aware of all new technology.

Throughout this book the term 'assistant' will be used to encompass various roles and titles for whom this book is relevant, such as personal assistant, executive assistant, business partner, secretary, management assistant, office manager, team leader and so on.

I have also used the term 'leader' as we are all true leaders whether we have the title or lead an actual team of assistants or not. We all lead ourselves, our bosses and our colleagues at some point to some degree every day.

It is also written for those who already lead teams or aspire to lead teams, giving you all the knowledge you need to be an effective and inspiring team leader. It is also extremely useful for anyone who is simply a team member and Chapter 4 in particular defines what a 'team' is and what a leader's role is within it. It will explain about team dynamics and the five stages of team development including the importance of creating a Team Charter using the example of 'Developing an internal assistant network'. I have also described ground rules for effective teamwork that can be included in the Team Charter.

Chapter 7 will explain how you can communicate with different personality and behavioural styles using techniques such as Transactional Analysis, TetraMap® behavioural profiling and Belbin® Team Roles. This chapter has insights and tips to enable excellent communication and to help avoid conflict and promote healthy teamwork.

Chapter 1 is about 'The leadership challenge' and it explains the styles that leaders can use and the strengths, skills and behaviours required to be effective leaders. There are tips on how to motivate yourself and others, how to empower and delegate, and how to make decisions both on an individual basis and within groups.

You will find out exactly what thinking strategically is and how you can develop your strategic thinking to help you, your boss, your team and your organization. This book will particularly help those who have people reporting to them and why vision and values are so important.

The following chapters are peppered with tools and techniques based on neuro-linguistic programming and they are about the skills you need to motivate, negotiate, influence and persuade, as well as offering practical tips on managing and leading people and projects. The book will enable you to manage change for yourself and help others through change as well as increase your emotional intelligence.

It has a chapter on managing the performance of yourself and others that explains the processes and procedures for recruiting, from attracting people to managing their performance. It helps you to define or analyse the role of a 'professional assistant' and learn what the characteristics, attitudes, skills and behaviours are. You can also download a resource from my website that details a sample job description and person specification that you can use to help you when recruiting, or simply check your own skills, abilities, behaviours and attitude against.

There are tips on making inductions worthwhile and memorable using a structured induction programme so that you can help new recruits feel a part of the organization from the start. It will explain how to create a 'Standard operating procedures' binder to help everyone with the knowledge they need to do their jobs effectively, and also advice on best practice in coaching and mentoring others.

The book discusses the need for performance management and how to conduct appraisals, including tips for the appraiser and the appraisee.

With the help of this book your skills will increase, your output will excel, your career will flourish, relationships will succeed and communication skills will be exceptional, which all enable the bottom line of the company to increase. You will develop the ability to lead yourself and your team, think strategically, check your values and be an example to others.

For most chapters there will be a bonus reference to extra resources for you to be able to download from my website **www.suefrance.com**. All you need is the password: BRR27110.

The book can be used as part of a training programme or when working towards professional qualifications.

I would love to hear from you and to hear your comments about my book(s). I am available for one-to-one coaching, delivering workshops, seminars and as a motivational speaker at conferences worldwide. I am always delighted to meet new people and I love travelling so please contact me at **sue@suefrance.com**. You can also connect with me on LinkedIn, Facebook and Twitter – I look forward to hearing from you.

Sue France

To download the free Resources mentioned throughout the book please go to **www.suefrance.com**; click on *The Definitive Executive Assistant & Managerial Handbook* Resources' page and enter the code BRR27110.

01 The leadership challenge

This chapter is designed to rethink leadership and explains that we are all leaders whether we have the title or not. We lead ourselves, our bosses and our colleagues at some point to some degree and on most days. I will explain the styles that leaders can use, the strengths, skills and behaviours required to be effective leaders. You will learn how leaders think, what they do and how they do it. There are tips on how to involve colleagues so as to keep them motivated, how to empower and delegate, and how to make decisions both on an individual basis and within groups.

You will find out exactly what thinking strategically is and how you can develop your strategic thinking to help you, your boss and your organization. This chapter will particularly help those who have people reporting to them, and explain why vision and values are so important.

Who or what is a leader?

Rethinking leadership

Leadership is primarily about people and relationships. You must have an honest understanding of who you are, what you know and what you can do. Also, note that it is the followers, not the leader or someone else, who determines whether the leader is successful. If the followers do not trust their leader or if they lack confidence in him or her, then they will be uninspired and unlikely to be influenced by that person. To be successful you have to convince your followers, not yourself or your superiors, that you are worthy of being followed.

Definitions of leadership

The only definition of a leader is someone who has followers.

(Peter Drucker)

To gain followers requires influence, integrity and trustworthiness, and if these are not maintained the ability to influence others will disappear. Leadership is a process by which a person influences individuals to accomplish an objective or a team to accomplish common goals:

Leadership is influence – nothing more, nothing less.

(John C Maxwell)

A definition of leadership by Warren Bennis is focused much more on the individual capability of the leader:

Leadership is a function of knowing yourself, having a vision that is well communicated, building trust among colleagues, and taking effective action to realize your own leadership potential.

After several years of studying what successful leaders do, Professor John Kotter of Harvard University has established that leaders engage in activities that fall into three categories:

- setting direction – providing a team with a vision, mission and a strong direction of how to get there;
- aligning the team so that they may believe in the mission and follow the strategies;
- motivating and inspiring team members (ie to put meaning into their efforts).

Everyone can demonstrate 'leadership'. You don't have to have a title to be a leader; you simply have to believe in yourself that you are the true leader you are. Twitter, Facebook, the internet and the breakdown of traditional hierarchical models have all contributed to changes in leadership. Progressive organizations need 'bottom-up' leadership fuelled by initiatives, new ideas and empowerment.

Leadership skills

You will find valuable information on leadership skills in other chapters in this book. *The Personal Assistant & Secretarial Handbook*, 2nd edition, also contains much information that leaders require such as how to set SMARTER goals, including a form that you can download in the appendix to structure your SMARTER goal setting and a downloadable Personal Development Plan, as all leaders need to continually develop, keep up to date and know where they are heading.

All team members, including leaders, have to be able to communicate clearly and concisely and in particular to lay out the vision, mission, goals and strategy of the team, department and organization in order for everyone to understand what the aims and objectives are. Clear communication will prevent misunderstanding, frustration and confusion and it will encourage motivation and a proactive attitude for everyone to aim in the same direction. A useful tool to help in this regard is the Team Charter suggested in Chapter 4, 'Leading effective teams to success'.

Effective communication occurs only if the receiver understands the exact information and meaning that the sender intended to transmit. Many of the problems that occur in organizations are due to misunderstanding that is probably caused by miscommunication as it leads to confusion and ultimately failure. It is the chain of understanding, between all team members, of what is being said and what is meant that makes a cohesive and collaborative team that produces successful results.

Communication is key and as such it will be dealt with in Chapter 7.

First understand yourself and then understand others

Understand your own beliefs and values. Seek responsibility and take responsibility for your actions. Search for ways to guide individuals and ultimately your organization to success. If and when things go wrong, do not blame others. Analyse the situation, take corrective action and move on to the next challenge. Also see Chapter 3 on 'Developing emotional intelligence'.

Leadership styles

Once you understand yourself, then you need to understand your team and how to interact with them. Successful leaders should be flexible and adapt their style of leadership and approach to their team members' needs, for task guidance and psychological support, via the following four styles of leadership (based on Situation Leadership Styles by P Hersey):

- **Direct:**   High need for task guidance
  Low need for support
  The leader defines the roles of the individual or group and provides the what, how, when, and where to do the task.

- **Coach:**   High need for task guidance
  High need for support
  The leader is still providing the direction; he or she is now using two-way communication and providing the support that will allow the individual or group being influenced to buy into the process.

- **Support:**   Low need for task guidance
  High need for support
  Shared decision making about aspects of how the task is accomplished; the leader is providing less task behaviours while maintaining high relationship behaviour.

- **Delegate:**   Low need for task guidance
  Low need for support
  The leader is still involved in decisions, but the process and responsibility has been passed to the individual or group; the leader stays involved to monitor progress.

Another leadership model is by John Adair called Action Centred Leadership. It focuses on the group you are leading and their needs. Your job as leader is to meet their needs:

Task need:	Getting the job done – they need clarity and a sense of purpose.
Team need:	Building and maintaining the team with a shared sense of purpose with a shared culture by setting and maintaining standards.

Individual need: Developing the individuals in the team, knowing and valuing them, ensuring working conditions are fair and providing them with recognition, status and opportunities to develop in a way that will build confidence and keep them motivated.

These three needs overlap, and meeting any one of them will have a positive effect on one or both of the others. For example, meeting the individual's needs frees that individual up to participate fully. Building a sense of team cohesion helps tasks get done effectively; a sense of pride in achieving a task gives the team cause to celebrate.

Adair says to meet the team's three needs, there are eight functions you must carry out and these will improve your leadership. These functions can be learned, practised, observed and refined. They are:

- **Defining the task**: Set out a clear goal and objectives for your team. Ensure they understand what they are supposed to do.

- **Planning**: Work with your team to put together a creative plan that breaks the task into stages and lays out clear roles for team members.

- **Briefing**: Use your plan to build a shared understanding among your team. Communicate clearly, simply and in vivid terms. Use this opportunity to address individuals' questions and concerns.

- **Controlling**: Get the most from the assets and resources available, including the team. Gradually build self-reliance so the team members can control their own work.

- **Evaluating**: Constantly review performance and give timely good and bad feedback to the team and individuals against the objectives set. It will be motivating and improve performance.

- **Motivating**: For example, demonstrate your own positive motivation, recognize and celebrate achievement, build relationships, empower others, enable learning and create a fair and inspiring environment. (See more on motivation in Chapter 2.)

- **Organizing**: Set up systems and processes to help your team work efficiently.

- **Setting an example**: Decide on what message you want to give your team then live it. Set standards and demonstrate your integrity. Know your own values and ethics.

If you want to read more about John Adair's leadership model, you may be interested to read *The John Adair Lexicon of Leadership*, published by Kogan Page.

Leadership, vision and values

Vision

If you do not know where you are going, every road will get you nowhere.

(Henry Kissinger)

Creating a vision is the first step in a goal setting or planning process. While mission statements guide day-to-day operations, visions provide a sense of direction for the future.

> In their 2007 book *Leaders: Strategics for taking charge*, Warren Bennis and Burt Nanus wrote:
>
> *Leaders articulate and define what has previously remained implicit or unsaid; then they invent images, metaphors, and models that provide a focus for new attention. By so doing, they consolidate or challenge prevailing wisdom. In short, an essential factor in leadership is the capacity to influence and organize meaning for the members of the organization.*

It has been said that 'Managers are people who do things right and leaders are people who do the right thing.' The difference may be summarized as: efficiency comes from mastering routine, and effectiveness comes from the activities of vision and judgment.

At the heart of leading others is your ability to develop (possibly in collaboration with your team) and communicate a clear and compelling picture of your team or organization's preferred future. Visions create energy and paint the bigger picture of what could be; they can be emotional and spiritual and give a sense of direction and purpose. Our ability to develop an energizing vision and focus for ourselves, our team or our organization will determine whether we will be successful effective leaders. Goals need to be energized and focused by the larger perspective of exciting visions. Visions draw us forward to the future of our dreams and where we want to be.

Empower people through great software, any place, any time and on any device.
(Microsoft)

There's something going on here... something that is changing the world... and this is the epicenter (the late Steve Jobs of Apple Computers during its initial start-up).

Values

Values and attitudes play an important part in whether a leader is respected and followed or not. The most popular values are: integrity (being consistent in one's dealings with people and resources); respect for human dignity; the belief that the effort people provide is directly related to the meaning they derive from their work; and a passion for communicating ideas persuasively.

Leaders know what they value and recognize the importance of ethical behaviour and demonstrate these in their leadership style and actions every single day.

You must also know your organization's values. A company can become well known for its values when the entire workforce, at all levels, live and breathe the principles. For example if a company has the values of honesty and integrity to be used every day in everything its members do, these can be seen by everyone in the fact that they keep promises, have personal accountability and respect each other as well as the clients/customers. When every leader and employee in the company knows, understands and follows the values of the organization then it will be successful.

As a leader, it's up to you to know these rules and codes of conduct, disseminate them, follow them yourself and make sure you enforce them. Good leaders follow their personal values as well as organizational values by understanding what standards of behaviour are really important to them and their organization.

Once you understand or even help to create your team's or organization's core values, you can begin to create the right environment for your team and your organization. Leading by example is the best way to do this. It is what you do, not what you say, that demonstrates to your team what you care about. So, if your company values honesty above all else, then make sure you demonstrate that by being honest with everyone around you. If your company values honest and open feedback, then make sure you allow your team to communicate openly.

You have to establish and make known the consequences for team members who don't follow corporate values. For example, if you allow someone to come in late continuously without prior arrangement, that won't set a good example for the rest of the team and it could cause upset and conflict amongst team members. You have to be seen as being fair and treating everyone the same. You should also set up some kind of reward system for team members who consistently act according to the company values as this also acts as an incentive.

Reputation

Concentrate on how others may perceive you, and develop the right image and appropriate behaviours so that others want to follow you.

Be a good role model

You should be the type of person that other people look up to and would aspire to have as their 'distant' mentor (see Chapter 6 on Coaching).

Example is not the main thing in influencing others, it is the only thing.
(Albert Schweitzer)

Lead by example

Make sure you 'walk the talk'. Have you ever been disgruntled by someone coming in late or arriving back at work after lunch 15 minutes later than allowed; if you think about it – you have also been late sometimes (for very good reasons I'm sure). Have you ever criticized someone for being on social media in work time and found yourself doing the same? Do you have the mentality of 'Do as I say, not as I do?' No matter what the situation is, to see people saying one thing and then doing another always feels like betrayal. If you can remember a time when this happened to you, you can probably remember a sense of disappointment and a feeling of being let down.

If you are a 'leader', then you know that you have a responsibility to your team. They look to you for guidance and strength; that's part of what being a leader is. And a big part of your responsibility is to lead them with your own actions.

When you lead by example, you create a picture of what is possible and you make it easy for others to follow you. People believe that if you can do something, then so can they.

Leading a team of your peers is a definite challenge. It can put all of your leadership skills to the test: from setting goals to involving team members in decision making to creating a climate of openness and honesty. If you remember to put your team's needs first, and if you work very hard to protect their interests, you'll prove to them that you're committed to and passionate about their success. When you demonstrate that you believe in the value of their work, and when you're willing to work through any obstacles you encounter, your team will respect your integrity – and they'll want to work hard with you, and for you, to achieve results.

Employee involvement

Employee involvement is creating an environment in which people have an impact on decisions and actions that affect their jobs. It is a management and leadership philosophy about how people are most enabled to contribute to continuous improvement and the ongoing success of their organization. In this section we will discuss empowerment, delegation and decision making.

Empowerment

Empowerment is a great motivator and people are more inclined to work hard for leaders who empower them to accomplish great things. Being empowered means that you are trusted, and when people feel trusted they want to take on more responsibility and they work harder.

> As we look ahead into the next century, leaders will be those who empower others.

(Bill Gates)

When leading your peers, be creative with reward and recognition and give praise wherever it's due. Assigning a task or granting a level of authority would be perceived by some as a very effective reward.

Working in teams can be satisfying and productive when team members work well together. Without sufficient direction, teams may focus on the wrong objectives, fail to use important resources, be torn apart with avoidable infighting, and may fail, with sometimes dire consequences for the organization.

Experience has proved that we should involve people as much as possible in all aspects of work decisions and planning, which encourages their buy-in and cooperation. This involvement increases ownership and commitment, retains your best employees, and fosters an environment in which people choose to be motivated and contributing. It is also important for team building.

To get employees involved in decision making and continuous improvement activities you can include such methods as managing a project team, suggestion systems, taskforce teams, continuous improvement meetings and corrective action processes.

Empowering others is an integral part of getting things done efficiently, however uncomfortable you may feel about delegating. Once you get used to delegating and your confidence builds, you can use proactive delegation as an empowerment tool. Plan to delegate larger projects and more decisions. Where appropriate, include your team in delegation decisions. Allow people to have a say in what tasks they want to take on. This increases their motivation, empowers them and reinforces their value to the overall team.

The art of delegation

Common reactions when thinking about delegation are when you hear your inner voice saying:

- 'I know it will be right if I do it myself.'
- 'They will resent being asked, and think that I should do the work myself.'
- 'It's a boring job, so I will "lead by example" and do it myself.'
- 'It will be quicker if I do it myself.'

However, the belief that you can do it better and faster with fewer mistakes leads to a lack of leadership skills and a vicious cycle of too little time and too much to do. Team members may feel disgruntled because you are keeping all the work to yourself and it may lead to inefficient and ineffective use of time and even to a lot of unnecessary stress.

If you feel that when you delegate there is a risk of not having the job done properly, then you need to make sure you are delegating effectively. Successful delegation takes time and energy to help team members succeed, develop and meet your expectations. Delegating will help build the employee's self-confidence and people who feel successful usually are successful.

Tips for effective delegation

- Clarify your expectations. Tell the person to whom you are delegating what you need accomplished and why it's important. When he or she knows the desired results, it's much easier to see the 'big picture' and work accordingly. If possible, connect the task to organizational goals.

- Clearly identify constraints and boundaries. Where are the lines of authority, responsibility and accountability? Should the person wait to be told what to do? Ask what to do? Recommend what should be done, and then act? Act, and then report results immediately? Or initiate action, and then report back periodically?

- Understand that you can delegate some responsibility, but you are ultimately accountable.

- Provide adequate support and be available to answer questions. Ensure the project's success through ongoing communication and monitoring as well as provision of resources and credit.

- Focus on results. Concern yourself with what is accomplished, rather than detailing how the work should be done. Your way is not necessarily the only or even the best way! Allow the person to control his or her own methods and processes. This facilitates success and trust.

- Avoid 'upward delegation'. If there is a problem, don't allow the person to shift responsibility for the task back to you; ask for recommended solutions, and don't simply provide an answer.

- Build motivation and commitment. Discuss how success will impact financial rewards, future opportunities, informal recognition and other desirable consequences. Provide recognition where deserved.

- Establish and maintain control. Discuss timelines and deadlines; agree on a schedule of checkpoints at which you'll review project progress; make adjustments as necessary and take time to review all submitted work.

- If you can't delegate a whole task, make sure people understand the overall purpose of the project or task as they are more likely to contribute most effectively when they are aware of the 'big picture'.

- Make sure they understand exactly what you want them to do. Give clear and full instructions and don't assume that they know something. Ask questions to make sure they understand, and ask them to paraphrase back.

- Let them know it is okay to keep on asking you questions rather than spend an hour or two getting it wrong.

- Ask for periodic updates and feedback to make sure your instructions were understood. Identify the key points of the project or dates when you want feedback about progress. You need assurance that the delegated task or project is on track and if for any reason people cannot meet the deadline then assure them it's okay as long as they let you know in good time before the deadline so that you can do something about it.

- If you have a vision/picture of what a successful outcome or output will look like, then share it.

- Identify the measurements or the outcome you will use to determine that the project was successfully completed.

- Thank and possibly reward them for their successful completion of the task or project you delegated.

- Talk openly about consequences of missing deadlines and expectations and explain to them that you expect them to try and think of solutions to problems they encounter, instead of simply asking for more instructions.

- Understand that delegating requires enough time and support from you so that everyone can be successful. You know that delegation is a key part of empowerment, and your team is stronger because of it.

- Delegate larger projects to teams of people, giving them appropriate responsibility and clearly defining their authority for decision making.

Delegation is a time management strategy that you must practise. You can't do everything – so decide what you must do yourself and what you can delegate to others. When you learn to delegate effectively, you'll be rewarded with more time and a more empowered and satisfied staff. That's a win–win!

The most appropriate time to delegate

To determine when delegation is most appropriate ask yourself the following questions:

- Is there someone else who has (or can be given) the necessary information or expertise to complete the task? Essentially, is this a task that someone else can do, or is it critical that you do it yourself?
- Does the task provide an opportunity to grow and develop another person's skills?
- Is this a task that will recur, in a similar form, in the future?
- Do you have enough time to delegate the job effectively? Time must be available for adequate training, for questions and answers, for opportunities to check progress, and for rework if that is necessary.
- Is this a task that you should delegate? Tasks critical for long-term success (for example, recruiting the right people for your team) genuinely do need your attention.
- How much time is there available to do the job?
- Is there time to redo the job if it's not done properly the first time?
- What are the consequences of not completing the job on time?
- How important is it that the results are of the highest possible quality?
- Is an 'adequate' result good enough?
- How much would failure impact other things?

When you first start to delegate to someone, you may notice that he or she takes longer than you do to complete tasks. This is because you are an expert in the field and the person you have delegated to is still learning. Be patient; if you have chosen the right person to delegate to, and you are delegating correctly, you will find that he or she quickly becomes competent and reliable.

Decision making and problem solving

Decision making

Decision making is an essential leadership skill. If you can learn how to make timely, well-considered decisions, then you can lead your team to well-deserved success.

While many of the decisions we make on a daily basis are quite simple with little consequence, some are difficult and could have huge consequences. These decisions may involve assimilating a huge amount of information, exploring many different ideas and drawing on many strands of experience. The consequences of the right or wrong decision may be profound for our reputation, for the team and for the organization; therefore it is crucial that we have a framework to get it right.

The seven key steps to decision making are:

1 **Define correctly the real decision to be made.**

   It is easy to leave out important information that we require in order to make a fully informed decision because we start to filter things out and make assumptions based on our previous experience and our own personal values. To identify the true issues that the decision must address, the key questions to ask yourself are: 'Why am I making this decision – is the objective clear?' 'What has led to the situation that now demands a decision and what does it really require?' 'What will the consequences be of making this decision?' 'What will the consequences be of not making a decision?'

   Understand the real drivers of the need to make the decision and try and think of some initial options.

2 **Understand the context in which the decision needs to be made.**
   Each situation is unique. It is critical to do an analysis of the situation. Ask yourself what has been done previously in similar situations and what has worked? Who are the people involved? What are the key critical success factors? Who will be impacted by the decision? Who needs to be involved in the decision and in what way?

   To enable you to analyse the risks, you must strike a balance between the risk of the decision and the amount of information you have. Remember knowledge is power and you must have the right level of information to make an informed decision. Always err on the side of caution as usually what you know is a lot less than what you think you know!

3 **Identify the options.**
   It is often the case that a major difficulty is the lack of options, especially when the options don't address the needs. This could be the result of a lack of creativity or inadequate analysis that has not identified the real situation and what might be done to address the issues. You could get creative and brainstorm the options with your team and think of as many 'out of the box' options as you can – if you don't dream it, it can never happen! Get input from others

outside of the situation and develop your ideas. Don't think 'this can't be done'; think 'how can this be done?'

4 Evaluate the consequences of each option.
Decision making is about how to take reasonable risks. You now need to look at the different options and assess these risks. Reasonableness is subjective and will differ with each person. You have to find the most acceptable set of consequences, given your current context and desired goals. You should also consider 'What will be my level of regret if I do this and what will it be if I don't?' When evaluating, you have to consider deductive or inductive analytical tools. Deduction is when there is a logical flow of reasoning that leads to a 'therefore' conclusion. Induction presents a group of facts or ideas from which a conclusion can be inferred, and they are probably open to several different interpretations. You should also check out the benefits of the options.

The assessment of the consequences of your decision is about which option will produce the optimum result, in relation to the context and your objectives, of making your decision. It involves understanding the very real consequence of your decision.

5 Prioritize the options and choose one.
Most people find taking a decision difficult, if not impossible and will try to avoid or defer commitment. This arises from self-doubt or an unwillingness to be held responsible. Often an organization's culture encourages and reinforces such behaviour by employees and will determine the general tendency for people to take responsibility for decisions. If you have decided on more than one option then you have to prioritize them.

Having analysed, brainstormed and assessed your options, you should now have a list of possible ways forward. You need to commit to a decision, own it and ensure that you can justify the why and the how of your decision. Do you know what the consequences of each option is and is your reason decisive and convincing?

6 Review the decision taken.
The frequency and depth of the review will depend on the magnitude of the decision. There are three types of review: 'periodic', such as annual reviews, committee meetings; 'emergency ad hoc reviews', where something has changed or new information has emerged which warrants this, eg a disaster recovery meeting; and 'sequential

reviews' where other decisions are based on the outcome of previous decisions.

7 **Take action to effect the decision.**
Once a decision has been made it must be implemented. Where stakeholders have not been involved in the decision-making process you will need to get the buy-in to the decision after it has been made. Handle this extremely carefully or implementation can go wrong. Wherever possible those involved with implementing the decision should be involved with making it.

Thinking strategically

You may need to think strategically about the area you are responsible for and involved in, for example when managing projects. You may work for an executive who has the responsibility for organizational strategic thinking. Showing that you understand and helping wherever you can goes a long way to being a strategic thinker and leader. You can help executives by making sure they have the time and resources to think strategically – demonstrate your business acumen and show them your keenness to understand. If you understand what strategy is and can think in this way, then you will help the people around you to be more strategic and it will make you a better assistant, leader and team member.

Three different levels of strategy

- **Corporate strategy**: concerned with the overall purpose of the business to meet stakeholder expectations. This is a crucial level since it is heavily influenced by investors in the business and acts to guide strategic decision making throughout the business. Corporate strategy is often stated clearly in a 'mission statement'.

- **Business unit strategy**: concerned more with how a business competes successfully in a particular market. It concerns strategic decisions about choice of products, meeting needs of customers, gaining advantage over competitors, exploiting or creating new opportunities etc.

- **Operational strategy**: concerned with how each part of the business is organized to deliver the corporate and business-unit-level strategic direction. Operational strategy therefore focuses on issues of resources, processes, people etc.

To think strategically, you need to understand:

- What direction is your organization going in? What are the aims and goals to be obtained? Where is the business trying to get to in the long term? What is the vision and mission of the organization? What are its growth, size and profitability goals?

- What are the current strategies – planned or implied? Which markets should your organization compete in? Which geographical areas should it compete in?

- How can your organization gain an advantage and perform better than the competition in those markets? What kind of activities are involved in such markets? What is happening in the industry, with your competitors and in general? What external, environmental factors affect the business's ability to compete?

- What resources – skills, assets, finance, relationships, technical competence, facilities etc – are required in order to be able to compete effectively? What products and services will we offer? What technologies will we employ? What capabilities will we require? What will we make, what will we buy, and what will we acquire (through alliance)?

- What are the values and expectations of the stakeholders (ie those who have power in and around the business)?

Strategic analysis tools

There are several strategic analysis tools to help you analyse the strength of an organization's position and understand the important external factors that may influence that position. The process of strategic analysis can be assisted by the following tools:

- **PESTLE strategic investigation**: a technique for understanding the 'environment' in which a business operates. See Chapter 8 on 'Managing projects' and events for a full explanation of how to conduct a PESTLE analysis.

- **SWOT analysis**: a useful summary technique for summarizing the key issues arising from an assessment of a business's 'internal' position and 'external' environmental influences. What are the Strengths, Weaknesses, Opportunities and Threats?

- **Scenario planning**: a technique that builds various plausible views of possible futures for a business.

- **Market segmentation**: a technique that seeks to identify similarities and differences between groups of customers or users.

- **Directional policy matrix**: a technique that summarizes the competitive strength of a business's operations in specific markets.

- **Competitor analysis**: a wide range of techniques and analysis that seek to summarize a business's overall competitive position.

- **Critical success factor analysis**: a technique to identify those areas in which a business must outperform the competition in order to succeed.

- **Five forces analysis**: a technique for identifying the forces that affect the level of competition in an industry.

Tips to think strategically are:

- **Anticipate**
  Have 'peripheral vision'; think 'out of the box' and not just aim straight for the goal. To anticipate well:
  - look for game-changing information at the periphery of your industry;
  - search beyond the current boundaries of your business;
  - build wide external networks to help you scan the horizon better.

- **Think critically**
  Critical thinkers question everything. To master this skill you must:
  - reframe problems to get to the bottom of things, in terms of root causes;
  - challenge current beliefs and mindsets, including your own;
  - uncover hypocrisy, manipulation and bias in organizational decisions.

- **Interpretation**
  Make sure there is no ambiguity, take time to understand, validate what is true and discard assumptions. Analyse the different information from the different sources and:
  - seek patterns in multiple sources of data;
  - encourage others to do the same;
  - question assumptions and test theories simultaneously.

- **Align**
  A strategic leader must encourage open dialogue, build trust and engage key stakeholders, especially when views differ. You need to:
  - understand what drives other people's agendas, including hidden agendas;
  - bring tough issues to the surface, even when it's uncomfortable;
  - assess risk tolerance and follow through to build the necessary support.
- **Learn**
  Success and failure are valuable sources of learning. You need to:
  - encourage and demonstrate honest, thorough debriefs to extract lessons to learn;
  - shift course quickly if you realize you are off track;
  - celebrate both success and (well-intentioned) failures that provide insight.
- **Strategic choice and implementation**
  This process involves understanding stakeholder expectations, and identifying, evaluating and selecting strategic options; then the task is to put them into action.

Summary

Leadership and learning are indispensable to each other.
(John F Kennedy)

Now that you know you too are a leader in your own right, remember to make a vision for yourself and your team, think strategically, check your values and set the right examples. Explore new ideas, be fair and treat everyone with equality. You should take the opportunity to develop every day through interacting with others, learning from mistakes, reflection, self-study and formal classes.

You can achieve so much more by involving others, making the right decisions and delegating effectively. Remember to choose the right tasks to delegate, identify the right people to delegate to, and delegate in the right way.

Look at your strengths and build on them, look at your weaknesses and improve them, look at yourself and be proud!

How to motivate yourself and your teams

02

Motivation can be defined as internal and external factors affecting the reason or reasons anyone has for behaving in a particular way and the general desire or willingness to do something.

This chapter covers motivational theories by Tony Robbins – the Six Human Needs theory – Maslow's hierarchy of needs and Dan Pink's Autonomy, Mastery and Purpose. It will explain how to look out for the signs of demotivation and it will help you to understand how you can motivate yourself and others. It also includes tips on how to motivate your boss.

The heart of job satisfaction is in your attitude and expectations; it's more about how you approach your job than the actual duties you perform.

Understanding your own and other people's motives and reasons for doing something is the key to becoming a good employee, team player and leader. We need to understand how to create an environment where people are motivated – including ourselves.

In order to lead and motivate you need to be able to:

- understand and communicate the vision and mission of what the business stands for and where it is heading;
- demonstrate your values and priorities and the values of the organization;
- know what you as an individual intend to do, in order to realize that vision and reflect those values;

- learn what individual employees can do to realize that vision and reflect those values for themselves.

(See more on vision, mission and values in Chapter 1, 'The Leadership challenge'.)

A leader shapes and shares a vision which gives point to the work of others.

(Charles Handy)

Motivational theories

Six Human Needs theory by Tony Robbins

This theory is based on the belief that all humans have the same six human needs (drivers) and all are universal; everyone is – or can be – motivated by their desire to fulfil them. Our behaviour is an attempt to meet these six needs. If we don't satisfy them productively then we will satisfy them un-productively. It is a useful way to look at people's behaviours and a good framework for leaders to use to add more depth to their leadership style. Remember you are a leader of yourself and your boss even if you don't actually lead a team.

You may want to consider these needs when thinking about developing your team members or leading your boss and ask the question: 'what need or needs do my team/boss have that will enable them to fulfil their job roles effectively?'

The six needs

1 Certainty/comfort
  We all want comfort. And much of this comfort comes from certainty. Of course there is no absolute certainty, but we want certainty that our computer will start up, the canteen will be open when we want it to be and our job will still be there when we wake up tomorrow morning. When we arrive at work in the morning we want certainty, for example by expecting the telephones to work and other people to join us in the office. When we get total and too much certainty we can get bored and then we have a second human need.

2 Variety
  At the same time as we want certainty, we also crave variety.
  We all like surprises but only the surprises we want, not the surprises

we don't want! Paradoxically, there needs to be enough uncertainty to provide spice and adventure in our lives. Maybe we could do things in a different order, meet new people and grasp opportunities.

3 Significance

We want to feel special, unique, different and valued. Deep down, we all want to be important. We want our lives to have meaning and significance. Can you imagine looking back on your life and wondering whether you made a difference and coming to the conclusion that you didn't! Some people seek significance in a destructive way by bad behaviour and wanting to stand out, which can upset other people around them. They may continually be late for work or make a spectacle of themselves. Change their mindset and ask them to give their knowledge and work on a project to make them feel valued and significant to the team.

4 Connection/love

It would be hard to argue against the need for connection with other people. We want to feel part of a group or team. We want to be cared for and cared about. Abraham Maslow called it our need to 'belong' (see below). It's the essence of teamwork. It's what we crave for when we work with others. Some people may be solitary but they still have a need for a connection in some way – maybe with church or the community.

Everyone finds a way to meet the first four needs. The last two needs are the needs of the spirit, and this is where fulfilment comes from.

5 Growth

If you don't grow you feel bad – whether it's growth in development, or relationships. Life's not all about me, it's about we... There could be some people who say they don't want to grow, but that's probably because they have goals that don't inspire them (or no goals at all). To become better, to improve our skills, to stretch and excel may be more evident in some than others, but it's there. When we grow we feel we have something to give of value. We want to do something that makes a difference. Observe people and discover what needs they are seeking to satisfy, so that we can do things to make it easier for them to satisfy their needs, make them feel good and help them to set stretched goals.

6 Contribution

The desire to contribute something of value – to help others, to make the world a better place than we found it – is in all of us. Take that need away, and you lose all motivation. Human beings get excited to contribute once they have the chance to experience it and not just talk about it.

Evaluate the six human needs to better understand your personal motivations and examine which ones seem the most significant to you. Then, look at what you do to fulfil the needs of your boss and other team members. It will likely make a difference in what you do and how you do it. The second requirement is to know your map – the operating piece that tells you how to get there. People may want to meet the same needs for example significance but different people will do it differently.

It is possible to meet any or all of these six needs by changing either your:

- perception (belief or appreciation of...);
- procedure (vehicles or approach to...).

See Table 2.1 for examples of how a leader can meet the six human needs of a team.

TABLE 2.1   Examples of how a leader can meet the six human needs of a team

Certainty	Write a team charter together with the team (see Chapter 4, Leading effective teams to success) that sets out expectations of the team of each other.
Variety	Make sure everyone gets a chance to work on different projects and/or with different people. Maybe job-shadow for a day. Vary the tasks they do throughout the day.
Significance	Each team member brings unique skills to the team – make sure these are known, appreciated and awarded. Use their skills to help them shine. An important skill for a leader to develop is being able to appreciate team members aloud in front of the rest of the group. A simple thank you goes a long way.

TABLE 2.1   *continued*

Connection	Icebreaker activities can be conducted at the beginning of meetings. Make sure the team members have time to get to know one another by organizing team meetings and social events such as team lunches. Team-building events would be excellent, especially ones where they get to know one another's values and beliefs.
Growth	You can help a team grow by creating opportunities for quality discussion and knowledge sharing. Making available learning and development tools and techniques, whether through e-learning, scheduled classroom learning, being a coach or coaching others etc.
Contribution	Help groups connect with the overall purpose of the team. Create a mission statement so they know where they are heading and how they can help each other to get there. It helps if individuals see a connection between their own work and the success of the team and organization.

Maslow's hierarchy of needs

Maslow's theory of motivation states that people have five main needs and you must meet the needs in the following order of importance: physiological, safety, social, self-esteem and finally self-actualization. People are motivated by things that help them meet these needs. What motivates people will therefore differ depending on what need they are trying to fulfil.

The first stage of Maslow's needs is '*physiological*': these are basic needs and they are the requirements for human survival: that is, the need to eat, drink, work and sleep.

Many believe that the only reason we work is to earn money. Some people may be motivated by money and the opportunity to work overtime in order to pay bills or to save for their next holiday or car. There is no question that money, or what it buys (food, housing etc), is a prime motivator; however, money alone does not create the sense of fulfilment and accomplishment that many seek.

The second need is '*safety*': once the physical needs are satisfied, your safety needs take precedence and influence your behaviour. Safety includes the need for shelter, personal and financial security, health and well-being, including a safety net against accidents and illness and the certainty that you feel of keeping your job.

The third stage of Maslow's hierarchy of needs is '*social*' and involves feelings of 'belonging to' and friendship: for example belonging to an organization, group or team. We all need to feel a sense of belonging and acceptance. In the absence of these, many people can feel lonely.

The fourth stage comprises '*self-esteem*' needs: the need to feel good about yourself and to be recognized and praised for your achievements with a feeling of respect for yourself and from others. Self-esteem concerns your feelings of confidence, self-worth and the desire to feel accepted and valued and how you feel you compare to your peers. It also includes your competence and self-confidence. Deprivation of these elements can lead to an inferiority complex, weakness and helplessness.

The fifth need is '*self-actualization*': the need for personal fulfilment, mastery and recognition and realization of how you have grown and developed. The rewards you get and feel for doing a job well done. This need is the summit of Maslow's hierarchy of needs and unlike lower level needs, this need may never be fully satisfied as there are always new opportunities to continue to grow and continual self-development should be your aim.

The theory of extrinsic and intrinsic motivation

(Based on Carl Jung's psychology of the conscious mind as described in his book *Psychological Types*.)

Extrinsic motivation

Extrinsic motivation is when you are motivated by external factors that are given or controlled by others, for example by salary or by praise. Our jobs are usually based on extrinsic motivation, although there will be some intrinsic motivation involved if you enjoy aspects of what you do.

You may need an extrinsic motivator for doing your filing. This is something you may find boring but the extrinsic motivator could be the fact that you know if it does not get done, then your boss or you may not be able to find something quickly, thus wasting time and your boss may get irritated if it is not where it should be when he or she wants it. In order to avoid the boss's wrath, you make sure it is done on time.

Intrinsic motivation

Intrinsic motivation is when you are motivated by internal factors to meet your own personal needs. Most hobbies and leisure activities are based on intrinsic motivation. We do them because we enjoy them, not because we have to.

Even if we do a job we enjoy, problems can crop up where we need to do something that we don't inherently like – such as filing, speaking with staff about performance issues, completing reports and so on. We have to do undesirable tasks as part of our job, so we have to find a way to motivate ourselves to complete them. That's where self-motivation is necessary.

Intrinsic motivators tend to never procrastinate over a task and may even put off other tasks in order to do the ones they enjoy. To motivate yourself, you must examine and understand your needs, so that you know what you find valuable and rewarding. Then, by changing your environment and perspective, you can find the intrinsic and extrinsic motivation to complete those undesirable tasks. So, rather than relying on others to make a task more rewarding, you make it more rewarding yourself.

If you want to be more intrinsically motivated, you need activities that are moderately challenging – that stretch you but you feel you can do well, which will give you satisfaction.

Intrinsic motivational theory: Autonomy, Mastery and Purpose by Dan H Pink (2009)

Dan Pink (speaker and author of *Drive: The surprising truth about what motivates us*) developed the motivational theory of 'autonomy, mastery and purpose', and this epitomizes the very real concept of intrinsic motivation within all of us.

'Autonomy', 'mastery' and 'purpose' may seem pretty much common sense, but many managers forget how internal the drive to motivation may be. Pink's ideas may well identify why external motivators don't work effectively all the time.

Autonomy

Our default setting, says Pink, is to be autonomous and self-directed. Most management today conspires to change this setting from intrinsic to extrinsic motivation. To encourage intrinsic motivation, autonomy is the first requirement.

People need autonomy over task (what they do), time (when they do it), team (who they do it with) and technique (how they do it).

Mastery

While external motivation techniques require compliance, Pink says that real motivation requires engagement. Only engagement can produce mastery, becoming better at something that matters. Mastery isn't just the ability to be able to do things well; it revolves around being able to carry out optimal experiences where the challenges we face help us to grow and stretch our capabilities.

Smart organizations supplement day-to-day tasks with stretching tasks, not too hard but not too easy. There are three elements to this drive to mastery:

It is a 'mindset' – it requires the capacity to see the abilities you possess as infinitely improvable.

It is a 'stretch' – it demands effort.

It's 'progressive' – it's impossible to fully realize, which makes it frustrating, challenging and attractive, all at the same time.

Purpose

Human beings seek purpose – a cause greater and more attractive than just themselves – and businesses realize this. Purpose-maximization is taking its place alongside profit-maximization, expressing itself in three ways:

- goals that use profit to reach purpose;
- words that emphasize more than self-interest;
- policies that allow people to match their work with their passion.

These three ideas may well explain why many businesses can't get the most out of their people. They rely too heavily on the extrinsic forces to drive their staff, but people will always work with greater energy at something they themselves have decided to go for.

In summary, people get motivated and engaged if they feel they are in command of their own destiny in their roles, particularly while at the same time learning expertise and contributing creatively. So Pink's ideas add value to the motivation debate and allow us to see what is really driving people's performance.

Motivational theories, some of which I have covered above, help you to understand better what motivates and demotivates you, your boss and your team, and knowing this will help you to achieve your personal and professional goals. It is important for you to identify what motivates you and share it with your boss. If you are a leader then ask your team to identify what motivates them and make sure you discuss this with them.

Signs of demotivation

People who don't take responsibility for their work or actions are likely to have a negative impact on their team. Look for apathy, finger-pointing, missed deadlines or phrases like 'It's not my fault' to spot team members who are avoiding accountability.

To help people take more responsibility for their work, provide them with the skills and resources to actually do their job. Then set up an environment that makes it easy for them to change, and help them take responsibility for their decisions and actions.

You can do this by:

- ensuring adequate resources are available;
- communicating roles, responsibilities and objectives;
- re-engaging people;
- helping them take control;
- avoiding micromanagement;
- giving praise.

You can recognize when people are demotivated by observing, empathizing, understanding and simply keeping an awareness of what is going on around you.

Notice any changes in attitude or quality of work; there may be a lack of concentration or careless or incomplete work. Your workforce could be lacking in motivation if you have a high turnover, low productivity, a poor workplace atmosphere and a lot of employee grievances.

A lack of motivation can also be recognized by noticing if there is an increase in absence from work, increased sickness, arriving late into work or a lack of enthusiasm, and if people appear frustrated and possibly are not communicating well, if at all.

The 2011 UK Chartered Institute of Personnel & Development (CIPD) *Absence Management* survey report states that the number one cause of stress at work leading to absence is the volume of work given by management and people thus feeling overwhelmed.

What are demotivators in the workplace?

In addition to needs not being met as explained in the motivational theories above, here are some additional demotivators:

- change that introduces uncertainty, including stress and anxiety, in those affected by and those implementing the change;
- being under-resourced;
- listening to others who complain or try to avoid work, while you are working hard and they are not reprimanded;
- being given too much work just as you are about to leave for a holiday;
- being patronized or talked down to by colleagues;
- inequality of pay.

Remember that demotivation is contagious and can have a knock-on effect. I am sure you can think of more things that demotivate you but all of the above and more should be taken into consideration when you may be affecting others. Let's move on to understanding motivation more and what you need to do to help yourself and others, including your boss, with practical suggestions to help you be more proactive and motivated.

How to motivate yourself and others

Keeping yourself and your team motivated is a challenge and is crucial to the success of the organization. Unfortunately some people use fear to try to achieve results. This only works for a while and ultimately damages credibility. Motivating others is more about using incentives to influence people to motivate themselves.

When it comes to staying motivated, we are all different and therefore need different incentives. Some like a boot-camp style personal trainer to push them hard; others want an encouraging and supportive friend. For some, working first thing in the morning is perfect; others are night owls.

When you feel it is difficult to motivate yourself, think about what you are good at and what you have achieved. This builds confidence and confidence helps you motivate yourself.

Below are some example questions to help you motivate yourself and I am sure you can think of more. When you are motivated yourself you can then motivate others.

- My proudest moment has been when...
- The most difficult thing I ever accomplished was...
- Something I am good at is...
- The greatest thing I have ever achieved is...
- I have helped others by...
- The best decision I ever made was...
- Something I have learned to do recently is...
- If I want to I can...
- The most successful project I ever organized was...
- What happened when I motivated someone else to success was...

To help build up team morale, there are tried and tested ways to keep yourself and your team motivated. Find out what works for you and write it down on Table 2.2, which you will find later in this chapter.

How to motivate your boss

Bosses and leaders need to be motivated too. If you can do this, it will in turn motivate you and you will both feel energized, engaged – a win–win situation for you both.

Motivate your boss to delegate more to you, allowing him or her to free up time for other things. Your boss may not be aware that you are ready to assume more responsibilities and that you wish to take on new challenges, so be proactive; offer your help reminding them that you are there to support them. Don't wait to be asked to do it – take the initiative and take work from them, producing good work and showing them that you can do it builds trust so they will delegate more. You may be able to think of better ways to do the work and suggest solutions and ideas to make improvements. As they trust you more, ask for more challenging tasks that also motivate you to develop. Here are some practical things you can do:

- Compliment your boss when they do something they are proud of or have just made a successful presentation, or succeeded in winning a new client etc. Let them know how good they are – they need praise just as much as everyone else.
- Show your appreciation and thank them if they have explained something really well to you, have passed on an interesting project

for you to complete or have entrusted you with some confidential work. Talk to your boss and make sure you both understand and agree on priorities, based on what it will take to get the job done.

- Show that you care about your work, your colleagues and the organization, and of course about your boss. Find ways of working smarter and your boss will be thrilled that you can get more things done in less time, creating a better work–life balance. Remember to encourage and motivate your boss to have a balanced work and life as well, as this will promote health and probably better personal relationships for them.

- Value your boss's time; make sure people arrive at meetings on time by reminding the attendees. Make sure you remind your boss when to leave for a meeting so they are there in good time with all documents and papers required. Choose the right time to speak to them by observing their body language and listening to them. Keep time thieves away from them so they keep motivated and on target.

- Keep a positive attitude, be enthusiastic and remember to smile – it's contagious and when they smile back it changes your brain chemistry, making you feel good. Smiling is an underused business tool. No one wants to be around negative people – look on the bright side of things and look for solutions. If you want a positive relationship with your boss, be positive yourself.

- Show respect for your boss and make sure you show that you recognize their role of authority and adhere to their requests as much as possible. Be prepared to forgive them for any outbursts etc, and let them know that you don't take things personally and that you understand the pressures they are under.

- Prove you can keep confidences and are discreet. By building trust you can motivate them to have you as their confidant, knowing you will listen to them and keep it to yourself allows them to bounce ideas off you and also get things off their chest.

Motivational listening

Motivational listening is simply the act of motivating a person to action by listening to what they say. Here are a few tips to help you become an effective 'motivational listener':

Silence yourself

The simplest, most important technique for being a great active listener is not to interrupt or say what you think people are about to say by finishing off their sentences for them. Let the other person say what they need to say and give them time to think in the pauses. Do not feel that because there is a pause you need to fill the gap. Some people just need time to gather their thoughts and carry on. Of course you should still give off all the signs of listening and say things like 'yes I understand' or 'do carry on I'm all ears' or 'hmmm' etc. Remember too to use your body language and appropriate facial expressions, to nod your head as well as keeping eye contact (not staring!) and all the active listening skills you know. Sometimes people just want to 'let off steam' and then clear their heads and get to deeper feelings. If you jump in on the first sentence or two, you are cutting them off before you can understand what they really want to talk about.

Pay attention

Make sure you are focused on the other person and not looking over their shoulder to see who is walking through the door or looking out of the window. People need to know you are paying real attention to them or they will stop talking. When someone is talking, you must really pay attention. Think about what they are telling you and if there is something important for you to remember, then repeat that sentence over in your head to put it in your long-term memory instead of keeping it in your short-term memory; ask if it is okay for you to make notes if it is appropriate. Remember you should always have your pad and pen with you at all times, or you can use the technology available such as the facilities on your phone or tablet. Don't let your mind wander, and push away random thoughts that pop up in your head. Also, resist the urge to immediately come up with a solution but wait for the right moment and continue to listen to what they have to say. If you pay close attention, you may find another solution may arise that you can impart at the right time and in the right way.

Try to understand

One of Stephen Covey's habits in *The Seven Habits of Highly Effective People* is to 'seek first to understand, then to be understood'. This advice is so helpful and is worth remembering. It is not only about what is being said but it is also about what is being meant! These two things can be entirely different from each other, or at least the way you perceive the situation and what is being said could be different from what the speaker is trying to say. Before you start jumping into solutions and 'here's what I would do' advice, make a real effort to understand the other person's needs, wants and motivation. Remember that everyone is unique and different from anyone else; we all have different needs and motivators. Two people can be in the exact same situation and have the same problem but need very different solutions. By understanding first, you can determine the best way to help them.

Give advice from the other person's perspective (if appropriate)

Once you have listened, paid attention and really understood the other person, including what they mean as well as the words they use, then you can offer advice. Your advice should reflect the fact that you have empathized with them by putting yourself in their position and it should be from their perspective, not yours. They may have come up with some solutions and not be sure what path to take, or only have half solutions, but base your solutions on those. You should be objective, look at it from their point of view and give them the benefit of your advice now that you understand their desires, needs and long-term goals. Offer the advice knowing what their strengths and weaknesses are, and think about their particular situation and the constraints they have. Once you get to know people you can give customized feedback and what is going to work for them in their particular situation.

Assessing yourself and your own motivators

Using Table 2.2 further on in the chapter, consider if your motivators are being met both on and off the job, and how well your own job matches your motivational profile. Then list suggestions of how, where and when you can satisfy these motivators.

Achievement

Do you regularly review what you have achieved and set 'SMARTER' goals for yourself?

Achievement-oriented people like challenging tasks, clear goals and specific measures of success. They set their own goals and work collaboratively with their executives. They want to be recognized for their accomplishments and like working for an executive who appreciates their abilities. Opportunities for ongoing skill development and possibly career development are important to them. They also look for ways of continually developing themselves, whether it is by searching out feedback, reading, sharing knowledge, networking, coaching and teaching others etc...

Interaction with others

Most of us, and especially those in the professional administrative roles, are people oriented and like, want and need to continually communicate, build relationships and keep updated. We enjoy frequent and friendly interaction with others and like to communicate face to face, over the phone, by e-mail, text or via social media, especially when we have busy executives to take care of. We value relationships with colleagues, enjoy learning about other people and may extend co-worker relationships into friendships. I still have friends among people I used to be an executive assistant to 20 years ago!

Creativity

People motivated by creativity tend to value jobs that involve varied duties and opportunities to be innovative. They like to be creative and to have some autonomy over what they produce, and don't like being restrained. They may like to write blogs and articles and 'think outside the box'. They get bored with repetition and like finding new ways to do familiar tasks, and enjoy brainstorming sessions. Usually, they would rather be the one to get a project started than the one to handle all the implementation details. They work best for an executive who is open to new ways of doing things, one who recognizes the value of their ideas and encourages them to be creative.

Leadership

People can be motivated by being empowered and may run community groups or chair assistant-networking meetings. They like to manage projects with full autonomy. They enjoy making decisions and directing the activities of others. They find power interesting, and may find ways to seek out interaction with higher-level executives and possibly volunteer to take minutes at board meetings so they know what is going on in their organization.

They understand the vision, mission and values of the organization and department they work in. Promotional opportunities are important to them, and they want to be sure that their title, salary and perks appropriately match their position level. They prefer an executive who provides a lot of autonomy.

Support

Some people are largely motivated by the opportunity to help and nurture others or make the world a better place. They are good team players and like to help keep a conflict-free workspace. They need to feel that their activities and efforts ultimately have a positive impact on people and like to be appreciated and thanked for what they do. They are often attracted to helping professions, causes, charities or volunteer groups. They like to work with people who share their values and beliefs.

Problem solving

Tackling complex and challenging problems is a motivating factor for some people. They like the challenge and the feeling of satisfaction when they solve a problem. They can get bored with work that is too easy and seek out mental stimulation. They often enjoy providing advice and assistance to help others deal with both simple and complicated issues. Being seen as the expert in a particular field is rewarding for them, as they like to be recognized for their knowledge and expertise. They enjoy working for executives who appreciate their ability and who ask for help with solving problems. They are not likely to take a problem to an executive or anyone else without first thinking of a possible solution that they can offer.

Work–life balance

Having an excellent work–life balance means having time for your family and yourself as well as your career. You treasure and enjoy the amount of free time that you have to use as you choose and this helps to motivate you. You can re-energize yourself when away from the office so that you recharge your batteries and are ready to face whatever work throws at you. If you are a leader then lead by example and leave work on time, see your children in their school play, go to social events in the evening, take proper lunchtimes and encourage others to do the same. It is possible to organize flexible working and even home-working on occasion, and these things all lead to an energized, motivated and happy workforce. Are you motivated by your work–life balance?

Look again at Table 2.2, and enter your ideas in terms of the categories described above, and then consider how you fit in. If your job and your

TABLE 2.2 Motivating assessment table

Read the descriptions in the section on 'Interaction with others' and then, using the scale of 1–5 (1 being very low and 5 being very high), rate how important these motivating factors are for you. Then rate on a scale of 1–5 whether they are present in your job. Then list where you find these motivators in other areas of your life. If they are not present or you want to increase their presence, list where, when and how you can satisfy your motivators (ie what is important to you for your own motivation of life and how you can achieve them).

Motivating factors	Importance to you (scale of 1–5)	Present in your job (scale of 1–5)	Present in other areas of your life – write where	List suggestions of where, when and how you can satisfy these motivators and write SMARTER goals:
Achievement				
Interaction with others				
Creativity				
Leadership				
Service				
Problem solving				
Work–life balance				

profile are similar, then you should be highly motivated at work. If your job provides some factors but not others, you may have to meet those needs outside work, for example in your home life or by doing charitable work, writing articles/blogs, joining in with LinkedIn discussion groups or Twitter #adminchat etc. You could also satisfy your motivators by being a member of a voluntary networking organization such as European Management Assistants (EUMA), IAAP, AAPNZ, OSAP and the many other networking associations that you can find in each country around the world. Please look at Resource 1 for a global list of professional administrative associations.

Summary

It is human nature to have days where you are not as motivated as you would like; however, if you continue to surround yourself with positive and motivational people, those days will be minimized. It's important to have motivation in your life as it gives you energy to continue striving for your goals and a good feeling.

Motivation needs to be constantly worked upon and invested in. If you want to succeed and you want your team to succeed, motivate yourself, your team and your boss by using all the above tips and by leading by example.

The benefits of motivation are that there will be more fun and laughter in the air (which is motivating itself), and higher retention of staff and therefore less stress on trying to cover positions that are being recruited for. There will be higher levels of quality productivity with the increased use of innovation and creativity and therefore better results. A motivated workforce will gain an exemplary positive reputation among its members, potential employees, suppliers, customers and clients.

Developing emotional intelligence

03

This chapter is about emotional intelligence (EI) and how we can all increase our EI using empathy and emotions at work. EI is a skill of leadership that cannot be overlooked, because the primary skill of leadership management is to handle the emotions of others. Quite simply we are all human beings with emotional needs and EI has something to do with everything we think, say and do. Becoming more self-aware and learning how to make your emotions work for you in building more productive relationships will give you an edge in your career development. The daily challenge of dealing effectively with your emotions and the emotions of those around you is critical to your success. To this end, this chapter will also give you some neuro-linguistic programming tools and techniques, tips and advice.

> This chapter is applicable to each and every assistant, and remember when I refer to a leader – that means you! You don't need to have the title of 'leader' to be a leader. We all lead ourselves, our bosses and the people around us.

You need to understand and empathize with the team as individuals in order to be a good leader. You can also use the skills learned to help others lead too. After reading this chapter you will be aware of all the emotions we all go through, the ups and the downs, and how to read other people's emotions and control our own.

There are tips, tools and techniques from the field of neuro-linguistic programming (NLP), and more tips and advice using NLP can be found in different chapters in this book and in Chapter 1 in *The Definitive Personal Assistant & Secretarial Handbook*, 2nd edition.

Leadership and emotional intelligence

In *Primal Leadership: Realizing the power of emotional intelligence* (Harvard Business School Press, 2002), Daniel Goleman said: 'Great leaders move us. They ignite our passion and inspire the best in us. When we try to explain why they are effective, we speak of strategy, vision, or powerful ideas. But the reality is that great leadership works through emotions.' This emphasizes the need for high emotional intelligence to be an effective leader.

You should identify your emotional triggers – what gets you emotionally engaged? Once these are identified, you will be better prepared in future. It will take practice to begin having this control, and tenacity will help you avoid emotion at work and develop better relationships.

One excellent reason to use emotional intelligence is that studies of worldwide organizations indicate that people who score highest on EI measures rise to the top of their careers. Unlike your Intelligence Quota (IQ), which is typically fixed from birth, Emotional Quota (EQ) can be learned and developed and is critical to success in today's world. It's the single biggest predictor of success in the workplace and the strongest driver of leadership and personal excellence. So what are you doing to proactively develop your emotional intelligence?

Definitions of emotional intelligence:

- The ability to recognize that we have emotions, are able to name them and control them enough to enable us to choose how to behave.

- Emotional intelligence is the ability to understand and manage both your own emotions, and those of the people around you. People with a high degree of emotional intelligence usually know what they are feeling, what this means, and how their emotions can affect other people.

- Emotional intelligence is the principles and values that dictate the thoughts and feelings behind our reactions, which guide our response patterns in different situations.

To be successful it requires the effective awareness, control and management of one's own emotions, and those of other people. EQ embraces two aspects of intelligence:

- understanding yourself, your goals, intentions, responses and behaviour;
- understanding others, and their feelings.

Developing emotional intelligence (EI) in leaders

People are persuaded by reason, but moved by emotion; the leader must both persuade them and move them.

(Richard M Nixon)

Leaders often claim: 'Our people are our greatest asset' and therefore they recognize the value of having an engaged workforce. Understanding, developing and using EI enables leaders to have meaningful and effective relationships. It enables them to recognize and appreciate how decisions will affect people and how emotions influence everything we do. Leaders who are emotionally competent are able to recognize these different emotional patterns in themselves and others, and to direct them in appropriate ways.

Goldman, author of *Emotional Intelligence* (1995), claims that emotional intelligence is not new; Aristotle mentioned the importance of emotion in human interaction back in Ancient Greece:

> As Aristotle put it, 'Those who have the unique skill to be angry with the right person, to the right degree, at the right time, for the right purpose, and the right way' will have the edge in all aspects of life.

Those 'leaders' who lead without emotional intelligence might not be aware of the negative or demotivating effect that their style of leadership has on the people they are leading. Their level of emotional intelligence is often made apparent in the way they communicate with people.

We have long been taught that emotions should be felt and expressed in carefully controlled ways and then in certain environments and at certain times. This is especially true when at work, particularly when managing others. It is considered unprofessional to express emotion at work and many of us believe that our biggest mistakes and regrets are when we have had an emotional outburst.

R Caruso and Peter Salovey argue the emotion centres of the brain are not relegated to a secondary place in our thinking and reasoning but instead are an integral part of what it means to think, reason and to be intelligent. They show that emotion is not just important but absolutely necessary for us to make good decisions, take action to solve problems, cope with change and succeed. The authors detail a practical four-part hierarchy of emotional skills:

- identifying emotions;
- using emotions to facilitate thinking;
- understanding emotions;
- managing them and showing how we can measure, learn and develop each skill and employ them in an integrated way to solve our most difficult work-related problems.

There are four emotional skills that all the other emotions can be built around:

- **Identifying/perceiving emotions**
  Be able to read people and recognize how you and those around you are feeling. We must be aware and be able to accurately identify and recognize the emotions of others and be able to convey and express our emotions to others in order to communicate effectively.

  The initial, most basic, area has to do with the non-verbal reception and expression of emotion. Facial expressions such as happiness, sadness, anger and fear are universally recognizable in human beings. The capacity to accurately perceive emotions in the face or voice of others provides a crucial starting point for more advanced understanding of emotions.

- **Using emotions to facilitate thought**
  Get in the mood – how we feel influences how we think and what we think about. Emotions direct our attention to important events; they get us ready for certain actions and they help guide our thought processes as we solve problems. We let our emotions influence how we think and use them to facilitate thought – the ability to generate emotion and then reason with this emotion.

  Whatever we respond to emotionally is something that grabs our attention. We should learn to direct our emotional energy and thinking towards more important matters.

- **Understanding emotions**

  We need to find out what emotions mean for everyone and how we can predict how others are feeling and will behave. Emotions are not random events as they have underlying causes. The ability to understand complex emotions and emotional 'chains': the way emotions transition from one stage to another.

  Emotions convey information: happiness usually indicates a desire to join with other people; anger indicates a desire to attack or harm others; fear indicates a desire to escape, and so forth. Each emotion conveys its own pattern of possible messages, and actions associated with those messages. A message of anger, for example, may mean that the individual feels unfairly treated. The anger, in turn, might be associated with specific sets of possible actions: peacemaking, attacking, retribution and revenge-seeking, or withdrawal to seek calmness. Understanding emotional messages and the actions associated with them is one important aspect of this area of skill.

- **Managing emotions**

  Manage emotions with feeling and empathy – as emotions contain information and influence thinking, we need to incorporate them intelligently into our reasoning, problem solving, judging and behaving. This requires us to stay open to emotions – whether they are welcome or not – to choose strategies that include the wisdom of our feelings. Managing emotions focuses on how to integrate logic and emotion for effective decision making.

Each of the above four abilities can be isolated from the others, and at the same time each builds on the others.

Emotional intelligence has a part to play when assessing a person's potential for leadership. This is because emotions influence everything we do in the workplace. Managed correctly, they can lead to enhanced team spirit and increased output. However, emotions can also have the opposite effect on a workforce.

One of the biggest challenges for leaders is gaining or having the respect of the people who follow them. For a leader there are always challenges and hurdles to overcome. To meet these challenges, you have to be aware of your own emotions and the emotions of others. It has been suggested that observing the way people interact with their team members and other colleagues, on an emotional level, will give some indication of how they might act in a leadership role. This creates the opportunity to identify any development needed to boost skills and attributes, to increase their effectiveness as leaders and to help them learn how to modify their reactions to difficult and challenging situations.

Employees are looking more and more for a good work–life balance and for meaning in their work. To motivate and develop people in today's fast-paced and challenging work environment requires a leadership approach that recognizes and appreciates how decisions will affect people.

Leaders who use the concepts of emotional intelligence can therefore have a strong impact. By understanding how and why people react emotionally to different situations in the workplace, you can implement change more effectively as you will be more responsive to the needs and expectations of the people you are leading. Leaders with a high degree of EI will have complete trust in their staff, always speak kindly, listen to their team, are easy to talk to and make careful, informed decisions.

According to Goleman there are five main elements of emotional intelligence:

- **Self-awareness**: knowing your emotions.
- **Self-regulation**: managing your emotions.
- **Motivation**: motivating yourself.
- **Empathy**: recognizing and understanding other people's emotions.
- **Social skills**: managing relationships (ie managing the emotions of others).

Goleman states that the more that you manage each of these areas, the higher your emotional intelligence will be.

Self-awareness

If you are self-aware, you always know how you feel. And you know how your emotions, and your actions, can affect the people around you. Being self-aware means having a clear picture of your strengths and weaknesses, and it also means having humility.

To improve your self-awareness you could keep a diary and spend a few minutes a day completing it – writing down your thoughts in order to move you to a higher degree of self-awareness. At any time that you experience anger you have to slow down to examine why. Remember, you can choose how you react to any given situation, no matter what it is.

Self-regulation

People who regulate themselves effectively rarely verbally attack others, make rushed or emotional decisions, stereotype people, or compromise their values. EI is about staying in control of your emotions.

To improve your ability to self-regulate:

- **Know your values:** Do you have a clear idea of where you absolutely will not compromise? Do you know what values are most important to you? Spend some time examining your 'code of ethics'. If you know what's most important to you, then you probably won't have to think twice when you face a moral or ethical decision – you'll make the right choice.

- **Hold yourself accountable:** If you tend to blame others when something goes wrong – stop. Make a commitment to admit to your mistakes and face the consequences, whatever they are. You will quickly earn the respect of those around you.

- **Practise being calm:** The next time you are in a challenging situation, be very aware of how you act. Do you relieve your stress by shouting at someone else? Practise deep-breathing exercises to calm yourself. Also, try to write down all of the negative things you want to say, and then rip the list up and throw it away. Expressing these emotions on paper (and not showing them to anyone!) is better than speaking them aloud. It also helps you challenge your reactions to make sure you are being fair!

Motivation

Self-motivated people consistently work toward their goals and they have extremely high standards for the quality of their work. (Please also read Chapter 2 on 'How to motivate yourself and your teams'.) Motivated people are usually optimistic no matter what they face. Adopting this mindset might take practice, but it is well worth the effort. Every time you face a challenge, or even a failure, try to find at least one good thing about the situation. It might be something small, like a new contact, or something with long-term effects, like an important lesson learned. But there's almost always something positive – you just have to look for it.

Empathy

For leaders, having empathy is critical to managing their boss, a successful team or organization. Leaders with empathy have the ability to put themselves in someone else's situation. They help develop the people on their teams, challenge others who are acting unfairly, give constructive feedback, and listen to those who need it. If you want to earn the respect and loyalty of your team, then show them you care by being empathetic.

To improve empathy:

- **Put yourself in someone else's position**: It's easy to support your own point of view but take the time to look at situations from other people's perspectives.

- **Pay attention to body language** (yours and theirs): You know you have rapport when you are matching and mirroring each other. Also be aware others will read your body language and make very quick assumptions, so be aware of what is going on.

- **Respond to feelings**: Someone may ask you if you can help them out with some work, which means you have to stay late again. If it is really important to them you will be able to hear it in their voice and by their body language, so respond to the way they sound and appear. If you say you can't help on this occasion and you hear the disappointment in their voice, then try and find someone who can help, or arrange to go in early in the morning to help. Read their body language, facial expressions, listen to the language they use and respond accordingly.

Social skills

Leaders who do well in this element of emotional intelligence are great communicators. They're just as open to hearing bad news as good, and they're experts at getting their team to follow and support them and be excited about a new project.

Leaders who have good social skills are usually also good at managing change and resolving conflicts diplomatically. They're rarely satisfied with leaving things as they are, but they're also not willing to make everyone else do the work. They set the example with their own behaviour.

Thanks to the many challenges and opportunities that arise when working with others, leaders must have a solid understanding of how their emotions and actions affect the people around them. The better a leader relates to and works with others, the more successful s/he will be.

Take the time to work on self-awareness, self-regulation, motivation, empathy and social skills. Working on these will help you excel in the future!

By developing our emotional intelligence in the above five areas, we can become more productive and successful at what we do, and help others to be more productive and successful too. The process and outcomes of emotional intelligence development also contain many elements known to reduce stress for individuals and organizations, by decreasing conflict, improving relationships and understanding, and increasing stability, continuity and harmony.

NLP and emotional intelligence

Emotional intelligence embraces and draws from numerous other branches of behavioural, emotional and communications theories, such as neuro-linguistic programming (NLP) and Transactional Analysis.

For each of Daniel Goleman's five competencies we can identify models of neuro-linguistic programming that help to develop these skills as NLP takes this a stage further, enabling us to learn from emotions at the unconscious level.

I will first describe the basics of NLP and the NLP communication model to help you better understand the NLP models.

In relation to Daniel Goleman's five main elements of EI, I will map the tools and techniques that can be used in NLP against each element.

The origin of NLP

Neuro-linguistic programming was created in the early 1970s by Richard Bandler, a computer scientist and Gestalt therapist, and Dr John Grinder, a linguist and therapist. Bandler and Grinder invented a process known as 'modelling' that enabled them to study three of the world's greatest therapists: Dr Milton Erickson, father of modern hypnotherapy; Fritz Perls, creator of Gestalt therapy; and Virginia Satir, the mother of modern-day family therapy. They wanted to know what made these therapists effective and to train others in their methods. What is offered today as NLP is the product of this modelling process.

NLP consists of a set of powerful techniques for rapid and effective behavioural modification, some of which I have talked about in other chapters and some are outlined here. The operational philosophy to guide the use of NLP comes under four operational principles:

1 Know what outcome you want to achieve.

2 Have sufficient sensory acuity (clear understanding) to know if you are moving towards or away from your outcome.

3 Have sufficient flexibility of behaviour so that you can vary your responses until you get your outcome.

4 Take action now.

Understanding and using NLP, including being able to read body language, will help you develop your emotional intelligence, which means you will be better equipped to build rapport and develop relationships, as well as prevent conflict and misunderstanding.

Neuro-linguistic programming communication model

This model helps us to construct our reality – understanding what is going on in our worlds both physically and emotionally.

We are inundated with information through our five senses, and we code, order and give meaning to our experience in words, sounds, pictures, feelings, tastes and smells (our reality).

To describe the rich sensory experiences, past and present, we use language to attempt to convey it in words. Our language becomes a 'map' of the 'territory' of our constructed reality.

In order to reduce the overwhelming amount of information we receive and to be sane, we reduce and change the input of experience in three ways:

- **Deletion**: we leave out much of the input.
- **Distortion**: we change the input to make it fit our model of the world through the filters of our perception.
- **Generalization**: we create categories or classes from single examples, by chunking.

To communicate verbally, we repeat the process of deletion, distortion and generalization by:

- deleting or selecting information to put into words; or
- distorting by giving a simplified version that generally distorts the meaning; or
- generalizing by minimizing all the exceptions that would make conversation very lengthy.

Knowing these facts should make you realize just how easy it is for us to miscommunicate with each other, misunderstand each other and get mixed up with what is being said and what is actually being meant! (See Figure 3.1.)

FIGURE 3.1 Neuro-linguistic programming communication model

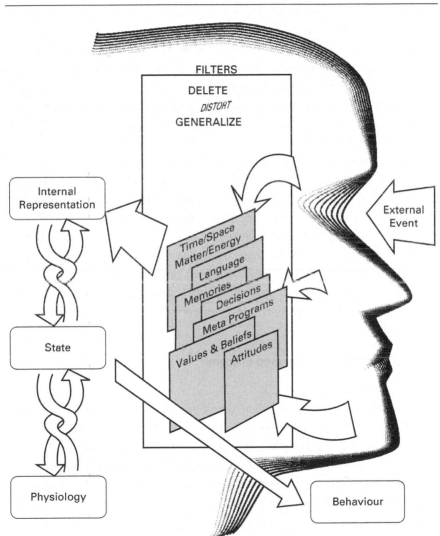

SOURCE: Reproduced from Tad James.

Emotionally intelligent NLP tools and techniques

Self-awareness

Beliefs

(You will find information and an example on limiting beliefs and empowering beliefs in Chapter 10, 'Change management'.)

Well-formed outcome

A well-formed outcome is an essential application of NLP as it is the ability to create and maintain an outcome that meets certain well-formed conditions. For example, my well-formed outcome as the UK Chair of European Management Assistants is to effectively lead the UK National Committee by coaching and developing their skills to enable them to be emotionally intelligent, chair regional committee meetings and run regional events for members whilst raising the awareness of EUMA, which in turn will grow the membership by at least 25 per cent by the end of 2013.

My well-formed outcome shows that I know what I want; that it is achievable and within my control; that I know when I will have achieved it as I will have 25 per cent more members; there will be no costs other than time that I will devote to this important mission and I have the resources I require – for example the knowledge and passion. The costs and consequences of achieving the outcome are well worth it as the organization has existed since 1974, operates in 26 different countries and is run solely by voluntary assistants in 'out-of-work' hours – amazing! Follow the process below and you will experience an improvement in your ability to reach your goals.

How to develop a well-formed outcome

1 What do I want?
   Ask this question about the context you are considering. State what you want in positive terms: what do you want, and what do you want it to do? Where do you want it? When do you want it? NLP emphasizes that you should strongly resist ever thinking what you DON'T want and always aim for what you DO want. What you think about is what you attract!

2 Is it achievable?
   Is it possible for a human being to achieve the outcome? If it has been done by someone, then in theory it can be done by you, too. If you are the first, find out if it is possible.

3 Is achieving this outcome within my control?
Can you, personally, do, authorize or arrange the outcome? Anything outside your control is not 'well-formed'. For example, asking your employer for time off is not well formed; the time off will only become well formed if it is granted.

4 What will I accept as evidence that I have achieved my outcome?
Is the outcome measurable? What evidence will you accept that lets you know when you have the outcome? Ensure that your evidence criteria are described in sensory based terms (ie that which you can see, hear and/or touch that proves to you and/or third parties that you have done what you set out to do).

5 Are the costs and consequences of obtaining this outcome acceptable?
Ensure that the outcome is worth the time, outlay and effort involved in achieving it, and that the impact on third parties or the environment is accounted for.

6 Do I have all the resources I need to achieve my outcome?
Do you have or can you obtain all the resources, both tangible and intangible, that you need to achieve your outcome? Resources include knowledge, beliefs, objects, premises, people, money, time.

7 If I could have it now, would I take it?
Are all costs and consequences of achieving your outcome (including the time involved) acceptable to you and anyone else affected by it? Consider the costs, consequences, environmental and third party impact of having the outcome.

Alternatively you can download Appendix 4 for setting SMARTER goals from **www.suefrance.com**, using the password in *The Personal Assistant & Secretarial Handbook*, 2nd edition. And there is a downloadable Personal Development Plan that has a SWOT analysis within it.

Self-regulation

Cause and effect

We have a choice to live in either 'cause' or 'effect'; although you may think things are inevitable, you need to realize that you DO have a choice in everything you do. Do you usually live at cause or at effect? (Consider the symptoms shown in Table 3.1.)

In NLP terms, cause and effect are linguistic patterns that clarify where two or more events are related in a way that one impacts on the other. The

TABLE 3.1   Cause and effect

At cause signals	At effect signals
You feel comfortable in your environment	You feel stressed in a particular environment
You can naturally say what you like	Others dictate what you say and when you say things
You act with a level of competence and abilities	You are panicking and questioning your abilities
You feel at ease, energetic and vibrant	You have low energy and feel overwhelmed
You are at ease to be yourself	You doubt whether you are good enough
You take difficulties and setbacks in your stride	You cannot say 'No' and try your best to please
Your choices are based on what you want	You do what you should do, not what you want to do

difference between cause and effect is one of responsibility/accountability versus one of blame (self) limiting beliefs and lack of choice.

Understanding the causes and effects of various emotions is an important element of emotional intelligence.

It is the rare individual who always lives his or her life 'at cause'; however far too many of us live a large portion of our lives 'at effect' – responding to the whims, desires or emotional states of others. Being 'at cause' means that you are decisive in creating what you want in life and take responsibility for what you have achieved or will achieve. You see the world as a place of opportunity and you move towards achieving what you desire. If things are not unfolding as you would like, you take action and explore other possibilities. Above all, you know you have choice in what you do and how you react to people and events.

If you are 'at effect' you may blame others or circumstances for your bad moods or for what you have not achieved or for your life in general. You may feel powerless or depend on others in order for you to feel good about yourself or about life – 'If only my boss, my colleagues... understood me and helped me achieve my goals or did what I wanted, then life would be great.' If you wait and hope for things to be different or for others to provide, then you are 'at effect' or a victim of circumstances. Believing that someone else is responsible or making them responsible for your happiness or your different moods is very limiting and gives this person some mystical power over you, which can cause you a great deal of anguish.

The internal dialogues that we go through often reveal the limiting beliefs that we hold as hard facts opening up outdated judgements and prejudices, distortions and generalizations or even other people's opinions. Listening to your own internal dialogues can help you to find the 'oughts', 'buts' and 'can'ts' that limit your own freedom of choice.

Here are a few examples:

- I am bored.
  How exactly are you boring yourself?

- Change is impossible.
  How is changing impossible?
  From what into what?
  Why is change impossible?

- I ought to do this.
  What would happen if you didn't?
  What would happen if you did?

- I just can't do this.
  What is stopping you?
  Why can't you do this?

- He doesn't like me.
  How do I know this exactly?
  What exactly does he not like about me?

- It is impossible to decide.
  How am I finding it impossible to decide?
  Why am I experiencing it as impossible to decide?
  What is preventing me from making a decision?

I try to live my life at cause as much as possible but it's not feasible all the time; however, at the 'effect' times I remember an NLP presupposition: 'There is no failure only feedback.' Then I endeavour to start living at cause again as I can now quickly identify when I am at effect and rectify it. Try it for yourself – there is nothing stopping you!

Remember you have control over what happens to you and you can learn to lead yourself!

Anchoring

This is the process of associating an internal response with some external trigger so that the response may be quickly, and sometimes covertly, re-accessed by activating the trigger. There is an example of how to do this in Chapter 10, 'Change management'.

Empathy

Sensory acuity

Notice what you notice, keep your eyes and ears open and be aware of what is going on around you. Once you know your outcome (goal) you must next have sufficient sensory acuity to know whether you are moving towards it or not. NLP teaches the ability to calibrate or 'read' people. This involves the ability to interpret changes in muscle tone, skin colour and shininess, breathing rate and location of breathing. The NLP practitioner uses these and other indications to determine what effect s/he is having on other people. This information serves as feedback as to whether the other person is in the desired state. An important and often overlooked point is to know to stop when the other person is in the state that you desire.

Social skills

Pacing and leading

The applications of this technique are many and varied. It is a good influencing tool. It can be used when people are upset, angry or defensive, or when you want to change someone's opinion at a meeting.

It builds rapport and relationships and shows you where rapport may be missing. When the quality of rapport is good it is possible to encourage an individual to follow the movements and thinking that you are using. Pacing and leading involves matching the other person's body language, and you can match breathing too (pacing) until you have gained a sufficient level of rapport and slowly start to change what you are doing, so the individual will follow you (leading). In this way you can lead your partner into different body postures naturally. Once you are in rapport, which is demonstrated by them following your lead, then your social skills increase and you are better able to build relationships, influence and persuade.

Emotional learning and transformation: reframing technique

EI has become an essential technique to understand in the business world. It is useful to be able to reframe your own thoughts and also help others to reframe their thoughts if you find yourself with a problem or 'faulty thinking'. Reframing is the process of making a shift in the nature of a problem. It is the process of changing a negative statement into a positive one by changing the 'frame' or reference used to interpret the experience (ie saying it in a different way and therefore thinking about it from a different angle). If all meaning is context dependent, and if you change the context or content, then you will change the meaning. All content can be reframed simply by changing the structure, the process or the context. The basis of reframing it is to separate the intention from behaviour and the consequence.

Almost all behaviours are useful or appropriate in some context. Interrupting a speaker by standing up and offering your view in the middle of a lecture may be judged as inappropriate. To do this same behaviour at the end of the presentation in order to provide a different perspective may be welcomed by all present.

A context reframe is useful for statements such as 'I am too pushy' or 'I wish I did not focus on what could go wrong.' In this type of situation, people have assumed that this type of behaviour has no value. Your job is to discover when it is of value by asking yourself the question: 'When or where would this behaviour be useful or viewed as a resource?' A possible reframe might be: 'Isn't that a great skill to have when you need to get things done or to avoid potential problems?' Once you become more resourceful, you can then assist them to discover behaviours that may be more appropriate in other situations.

If a person is involved in an undesirable experience, think of a new context, a different situation, in which the person will respond differently to the same behaviour or meaning. Ask, 'When else would this behaviour be effective?' Or, 'Where would this be an appropriate response?'

Example

'He is so pedantic in meetings; he slows us up.' (not good). 'Yes and doesn't he make an excellent finance manager spending the budget carefully.' (good)

If a person is involved in an undesirable experience, think of another meaning for the same behaviour that will change their response. Ask yourself, 'What else could this behaviour mean?' or internally think of an opposite frame or a different meaning. 'What is it that this person hasn't noticed (in this context) that will bring about a different meaning and change their response (behaviour)?'

Content/meaning reframe

The content or meaning of a situation is determined by what you choose to focus on. An electrical power failure can be viewed as disruptive, a major disaster given all you have to get done. Or it can be viewed as an opportunity to spend some intimate time with your spouse or to have fun with your children finding innovative ways to manage the situation.

A content reframe is useful for statements such as: 'I get annoyed when my boss stands behind me while I am working.' Notice how the person has taken the situation and given it a specific meaning – which may or may not be true – and in so doing limits their resourcefulness and possible courses of action. To reframe this situation, there is an NLP presupposition that says: 'Every behaviour has a positive intention' and therefore ask questions such as:

- What other meaning could the boss's behaviour have? Or for what purpose does he or she do it? A possible reframe might be: 'Is it possible they want to help and do not know how to offer their assistance in any other way?'

- What is the positive value in this behaviour? The positive value could be related to the boss's behaviour (as above) or it could be related to the speaker's behaviour. A possible reframe might be: 'Isn't it great that you know your boundaries and are not prepared to allow someone to violate them?'

Examples

'My boss just leaves me to get on with it; he never pays me any attention.' (not good)
Can be reframed as: 'He must really trust you and rely on you to do a good job. I wish my boss was like that.' (good)

'This organization is always sending you on courses. You never have time to get anything done.' (not good)
Can be reframed as: 'Wow! What wonderful development opportunities there are! Do you think I can get a job there?' (good)

Steps towards better performance using emotional intelligence

Here are a few suggestions to improve you and your team's performance:

Be emotionally attractive

Focus on being emotionally attractive. Cultivate the ability to manage your own emotions and to influence those of others in a manner that drives the success of teams and organizations. Try and create a positive emotional tone in the organization and engage and inspire people. You should possess the three core qualities of mindfulness, hope and compassion.

Look for good in others

One of the main objectives of a leader is to make sure others are aware of the greatness that lies in them. Be known in your organization as someone who is always on the lookout for what is right with people. It promotes goodwill and is good for business.

Be pleasant and cooperative

If all team members throughout the organization had these qualities wouldn't life be wonderful? If you are one of the team members who may not have it right yet, then you are halfway there simply by reading this chapter. Work on it and it will get you far. If you are a team leader then EI is imperative; it is almost impossible to have executive presence without it. For example sharing ideas and short cuts, helping each other out, coaching and mentoring each other – it all helps. This is another example of how moods and emotions affect productivity.

Model meeting behaviour

Take an honest look at your behaviour in meetings. Do you set a positive tone from the start? Or is it about however you are feeling at the time? Control your emotions and aim for a calm, relaxed mood, and a consistent, positive approach.

Emotionally intelligent thoughts

Think about a time when you felt really angry, upset or sad. Remember what you saw, heard, felt. Are there any smells or tastes associated with the memory? Really get those feelings in your head of how you felt at that time, hear what you heard, feel what you felt when you were really really angry, upset or sad. Once you feel the emotions rising up inside you, I now want you to calm yourself down, bring yourself back into this peaceful and happy time where the world is good and pleasant. Now, know that it was in the past and it is not now worth your time and energy focusing on it – let it go!

Bring forward good, happy, pleasant thoughts and feelings. I always think of my granddaughter Bella when I want to change my mood and be in a happy moment where I can't help but smile. Find out what it is for you that makes you feel happy. Calm yourself down and bring your mind back to a peaceful world where everything is good. You have now started on your road to becoming an expert in becoming emotionally intelligent.

Now think of this example: You are at work and a colleague (who has been hankering after your job for a few months now) has noticed that you have made a couple of errors in a document that is lying on your desk and starts to point them out loudly as your boss walks out of their office. The natural internal response would of course be to get angry with this colleague, especially as they have their own agenda in mind (ie working for your boss). It is at this point that you have to remember how to bring your temper down to a calm peaceful place and, without showing your anger to the person, calmly point out with a genuine smile, that you had already noticed the errors as soon as you had printed it as you always check your work before handing it over; thank your colleague for pointing it out and say you appreciate it. It is easy for tempers to fly, especially if you are busy and you feel people are interfering for no good reason and you can feel your blood starting to boil. It can take all your effort to keep control but this is what emotional intelligence is about – keeping in control, choosing our response rationally.

Summary

Understanding emotional intelligence enables us to increase our ability to control our own emotions and understand and support the emotions of others. This skill results in increased cooperation and a healthy work environment. Practise using the tools and techniques so they become second nature; they will help you become 'emotionally attractive' and in full control of your emotions. Remember to have emotionally intelligent thoughts, notice what you notice, and live at cause and not effect. You now have the edge to boost your career and home life and are also equipped to help those around you.

Use your emotional intelligence to improve communications and relationships, have better empathy skills, act with integrity, gain respect from others, manage change more confidently and have a more peaceful existence whilst feeling healthier and happier. Understand how you can help others use EI and help to reduce their stress levels.

Leading effective teams to success

04

This chapter will define what a 'team' is and what a leader's role is within a team. It will explain team dynamics and the five stages of team development, including the importance of creating a Team Charter, using the example of 'Developing an internal assistant network'. With the kind permission of Belbin® Associates, Belbin® team roles are explained so you can read the descriptions and determine what your preferred behavioural style is, together with each style's strengths. This will enable you to form well-balanced and productive teams. It also describes what each team role's allowable weakness and non-allowable weakness are so that you can be aware of how you can reduce your weaknesses where possible. I have also laid out ground rules for effective teamwork that can be included in the Team Charter.

Definition of a team

A team is two or more people working together inter-dependently, who have the same purpose and goals and work towards achieving a shared objective. They have the complementary skills necessary to carry out that purpose successfully together.

We all work in teams in our organizations, whether we are working with one boss or more and alongside our colleagues in departments. You may lead a team or have led a committee or task force, organized an event with a team or have coordinated a group of people to achieve a common goal. This chapter is about giving you the tools and techniques to lead effective teams, including your boss, for a successful outcome.

Internal networks are invaluable to your success, and not only to prevent reinventing the wheel but to share knowledge and have outstanding support for each other. You may lead an assistant networking team within your company, and if you haven't got one yet then I suggest you think about organizing one and becoming its team leader. There is a section below on how to develop an internal assistant network.

> *We are all guilty of not taking breaks when we should and rarely get an opportunity for training sessions or networking with colleagues. One thing that I have found that successfully remedies this, is to organize a network for like-minded people (Assistants and Office Managers). Continuous communication can do wonders for staff morale and at the same time build relationships with your colleagues, share knowledge and solve problems.*
> (Catherine Thomas, PA for the Director of Shared Services Partnership, NHS Wales)

Team-leader role

All the best teams need good direction. As a team leader, it's your role to help your team to work together to get the best results and help the business run smoothly. You should play a vital role in creating and maintaining a high-performance team, which is key to running a successful business.

Your duties will vary depending on the type and size of the organization/ team and who and how many you are leading. Your workload may involve managing processes, managing change, delegating tasks, monitoring the team's performance and motivating them, organizing and chairing meetings, organizing training and development, completing paperwork and handling complaints. It may involve working with budgets, stock ordering and taking part in special events. You may have to deal with team disputes and handle conflict management. You could also have wider duties like human resource matters such as dealing with sickness absence, return to work interviews, interviewing and selection, performance management, induction of new staff, acting as coach and mentor, reporting to senior level management and more.

As a team leader you need to understand what motivates the people who work with you – please see Chapter 2 on 'How to motivate yourself and your teams'.

Team dynamics

Successful team members can improve team dynamics by doing the following:

- forming teams in which members complement each other's strengths and weaknesses;
- understanding yourself: work style, communication preferences and team interaction preferences;
- understanding the people you work with: both internal and external to your organization;
- looking for ways to emphasize similarities and capitalize on differences between you and the people you work with.

Potential problems when working in teams

- It takes longer to make decisions with more people involved.
- There are more people and therefore more possibilities for disagreements.
- There may be personality conflicts.
- Miscommunication can happen.
- Individuals have conflicting goals or priorities and their own agenda.
- There may be insufficient sharing of information.
- Inappropriate/unproductive or boring meetings are common.
- The leader makes most of the decisions.
- Lack of trust can arise.

Benefits of working in teams

- Higher-quality decisions come from better ideas and higher-quality information.
- There is more creativity and innovation in solving problems.
- Productivity increases due to division of responsibilities.

- Job satisfaction is enhanced by team member interaction and greater accomplishments.
- There are social benefits. The team can provide a sense of community and camaraderie.
- It encourages networking. Team members can get to know their colleagues better.
- Team members gain visibility by showcasing their skills and talents for senior executives monitoring the team's progress.

The benefits of working in teams can be summarized as 'synergy' – the whole is greater than the sum of the parts. As a team, we can do much better work than when working individually and accomplish more with better results. Working in effective teams can have its problems but these are far outweighed by the benefits.

Characteristics of effective teams

The acronym T E A M W O R K summarizes the effective characteristics of working in teams:

TRUST:	Trust is the foundation of teamwork. Effective teams cultivate and maintain trust among members. Team members have faith in each other to honour their commitments, maintain confidence, support one another and generally behave in a consistent and predictably acceptable fashion.
EFFORT:	Teamwork requires hard work and energy to communicate and coordinate among members.
ATTITUDE:	Teamwork requires a facilitative/helping mindset. This means that team members are flexible in providing leadership at certain times and supporting team decisions at others. Team members see themselves as belonging to a team rather than as individuals who operate autonomously. They are committed to goals above and beyond their personal goals.

MOTIVATION:	Team members are motivated to collaborate rather than compete with one another.
WIN–WIN:	Team members strive to reach win–win solutions that satisfy all team members.
OPEN COMMUNICATION:	Team members communicate openly and honestly with one another. Communication refers to the style and extent of interaction – among members and between members and those outside the team. It also refers to the way that members handle conflict, decision making and day-to-day interactions.
RESPECT:	Team members respect and value the differences among members, including diverse views, expertise and backgrounds.
KNOWLEDGE:	Team members share knowledge and avoid reinventing the wheel.

Stages of team development

Psychologist Bruce Tuckman (1965) described the path to high performance that most teams go through as 'Forming, Storming, Norming and Performing'. Later, he added a fifth stage that he called 'Adjourning' although I prefer to call it 'Mourning' as it is the way I feel once I have worked well with a team and have bonded to such an extent I don't want to break the team up.

Reading Chapter 7, 'How to communicate with different personality and behavioural styles', will help in understanding people's behaviours and actions during team-development stages. The five stages of team development that help groups transform into successful high-performing teams are described in detail below:

Stage 1: Forming

If you can select your team or team members going forward, think about the various areas of skills and knowledge that you need as well as behavioural styles and in particular Belbin® team roles (see below). At the very least you should have individual face-to-face meetings with every member of the team to find out their wants and needs, and what they hope the team will achieve, and also to find out what experience, knowledge and skills they can bring and how they prefer to work.

When teams first get together they initially go through a 'Forming' stage in which members are on their best behaviour and are positive, cordial and polite. Beneath their calm and professional exterior however, they are sizing each other up and forming opinions (rightly or wrongly). They have unclear objectives and they avoid conflict. This stage is usually fairly short and may only last for one or two meetings at which people are introduced to one another and start to get to know and understand each other. At this stage there may be discussions about how the team will work, which can be frustrating for some members who simply want to get on with the team task. Some team members experience anxiety, try to get a feel for the situation, test to see what behaviour is appropriate or inappropriate, and check to see how much help or assistance can be provided by the leader or boss. Others are simply excited about working in the team and what it may involve.

As team leader, you have an important role to play in managing first impressions so as to make sure the team has the best possible chance of success. It is often how the leader behaves that dictates the chances of success. At this stage, you have a dominant role and make most of the decisions whilst other members' roles and responsibilities are less clear. Listen patiently to concerns, emphasize that the team is needed and be prepared to answer lots of questions about the team's purpose, objectives and external relationships.

Stage 2: Storming

Reality sets in and your team moves into a 'Storming' phase. It is important to realize that this will be followed by a normal phase of team development. As team members become more comfortable, they feel free to express differences of opinion. Your authority may be challenged as others claim their position, their roles are clarified and the ways of working start to be defined. Members compete with each other for power and are more willing to confront things they disagree with. As leader, you must be aware that some members may feel overwhelmed by how much there is to do or are uncomfortable with the approach being used. You should work at understanding people rather than judging them. Some may react by questioning how worthwhile the goal of the team is and by resisting taking on tasks. This is the stage when many teams fail, and even those that stick with the task may feel that they are on an emotional roller coaster as they try to focus on the job in hand without the support of and established processes or relationships with their colleagues.

It is important to note that at this stage the leader may be perceived as under-performing, unable to keep control and less dynamic than the team first thought s/he was. You may therefore find yourself challenged by the group. Although it can feel like a looming disaster, it is actually a sign of progress because a group with no disagreement will inevitably fail. It is important to remember that constructive conflict can improve decision making, it allows greater diversity and innovation and it avoids 'group think'. So as long as you know that this stage will be coming, you can anticipate it and give answers to questions that you think they may ask before they even ask them, proactively lead from the front and deal with situations as they arise.

Please note that not all teams will go through this process, but many will. It is important therefore to mention that as there usually is a 'Storming' phase in some form, you have to make sure that team members do not use knowledge of the 'Storming' stage as an excuse to behave inappropriately!

Stage 3: Norming

Gradually, the team moves into a 'Norming' stage, as a hierarchy is established. Team members come to respect your authority as a leader, and others show leadership in specific areas. There will be greater team cohesion and a willingness to actively listen to each other without confrontation. Now that the team members know each other better, they may be socializing together, and they are able to ask each other for help and provide constructive criticism. The team develops a stronger commitment to the team goal, and you start to see good progress towards it. There is often a prolonged overlap between Storming and Norming behaviour. As new tasks come up, the team may lapse back into typical Storming stage behaviour, but this eventually dies out and there is more of a sharing of ideas and the level of trust increases. This process is helped by the pressure to produce results. If you get new members of the team joining at this stage, be aware that they may challenge what is in place and a step back to Storming may occur.

Allow roles within the team to evolve naturally: each member of the team needs to play his or her role for the whole team to be effective. Take advantage of each person's unique strengths and avoid unreasonable exposure to individual weaknesses. Look for ways to bring out the best in those who may lack skills or experience. Motivate by being a positive force, even in negative situations.

Stage 4: Performing

When the team reaches the 'Performing' stage, hard work leads directly to progress towards the shared vision of their goal, supported by the structures and processes that have been set up. Members will now be working together productively and accomplishing team goals. To stay motivated, they need to feel that their task is meaningful and that they have the resources to succeed. They will be equally focused on the task and people and have a common purpose. Morale will be high and they will be motivated to share accountability and cooperate fully with each other. There will be an air of supportive group decision making.

As leader, you are able to delegate much of the work and can concentrate on developing team members. Being part of the team at this stage feels 'easy' compared with earlier on.

Project teams exist only for a fixed period, and even permanent teams may be disbanded through organizational restructuring. As team leader, your concern is both for the team's goal and the team members. Look at what works well and continue to do those practices. Continually develop the team and look at what you can do to keep on improving performance.

The only certain thing in life is change. At some point teams will change, members will leave and new members will join and successful groups will keep the momentum going with a leader who can effectively guide them through change.

A leader should encourage suggestions from the team and build a sense of joy and fun for the team, perhaps incorporating social activities, stress busters and outings to build team cohesiveness and celebrate successes.

Stage 5: Mourning

The 'mourning' stage is important in reaching both team goal and personal conclusions.

Some teams are ongoing while others finish their project or task and move on. The break-up of the team can be hard for members who like routine or who have developed close working relationships with other team members, particularly if their future roles or even jobs look uncertain. For project-based teams, the last stage involves dissolution of the team, which can be difficult for team members who are loyal to the team and want it to carry on. It is important to reflect on performance and evaluate it, possibly writing a report for others to learn from. Celebrate achievements and allow time for personal goodbyes.

As a team leader, make sure that you leave plenty of time to coach team members through each stage. Therefore you need to identify which stage your team is at from the descriptions above. So once your team has 'Formed' you need to consider what you can do to effectively move your team towards the Performing stage. You will need to schedule regular reviews of where your team is and keep adjusting your behaviour and leadership approach to suit the stage your team has reached and make sure you are doing the right thing at the right time. It may be that your team is a project team with a start and an end and therefore you have to take into consideration how you can celebrate the end of a successful project team.

Creating a Team Charter using 'Developing an internal assistant network' as an example

Team Charters help your team in the 'Forming' stage of developing a team and helps to make sure that everyone is focused on the right things from the start. Drawing up a Team Charter can also be useful if a team is in trouble and people need to regain their view of the 'big picture'.

Team Charters are documents that define the purpose of the team, how it will work, and what the expected outcomes are. It will make sure that all involved are clear about the direction in which they are heading.

The precise format of a Team Charter can vary in each situation and from team to team. However, much of the value of the Charter comes from thinking through and agreeing the various elements. Time taken agreeing a Team Charter will be well worth it as the team progresses.

Planning the Charter will help to speed the processes of Forming, Storming and Norming so that the team can effectively perform sooner.

The following are suggestions for inclusion in a Team Charter:

● context;

● mission, goals and objectives;

● roles and responsibilities;

● authority and boundaries;

- resources and support;
- operations;
- seven ground rules for effective teamwork;
- negotiation and agreement.

Context

This is the introduction to the charter. It sets out why the team was formed, the problem it's trying to solve (if appropriate), how this problem fits in with the broader objectives of the organization, and the consequences of the problem going unchecked.

- What problem is being addressed (if any)?
- What result or delivery is expected?
- Why is this important?

Example context when setting up an internal networking team of assistants:

The team has been formed to increase cooperation and cohesion between assistants who work within the organization, no matter in which department or whom they work for. The historic lack of cooperation between assistants has meant that they have reinvented the wheel on many occasions, have lacked support, wasted time and prevented productivity and has sometimes caused stress and missed deadlines. This has cost the organization money and sometimes has meant recruiting new people. The network team including the Team Charter helps to give team members a sense of belonging to a supportive team.

Mission, goals and objectives

The mission and objectives are at the heart of the Charter. By defining a mission, the team knows what it has to achieve. Without a clear mission, individuals can too easily pursue their own agendas independently of, and sometimes irrespective of the overall goal.

For example: Sharon Severn, secretary/PA to Bob Stoddart at Rolls-Royce plc, worked with her team and together they developed the following mission statement for their team to work towards:

The mission of this team is to work cohesively, sharing knowledge, advice, tools and techniques to improve meeting deadlines and producing excellent work. We will work closely as a team in order to exceed expectations of our boss(es), internal and external clients/customers.

Goals and objectives

The next stage is to take the mission and turn it into measurable goals and objectives. These are the critical targets and milestones that will keep the team on track.

Example goals for 'Developing an internal assistant network'

- *To interview all assistants to find out what they would like from the Team Charter and what ground rules they would like to be included by 31 December.*
- *To survey all executives to find out what they would like to be included in the Team Charter for their assistants to be able to help each other by 31 December.*
- *To present first draft proposals by 31 January.*
- *To hold a face-to-face meeting with all assistants to agree on the Team Charter by 28 February.*

Roles and responsibilities

Teams are most effective when they have members with the skills and experience needed to do the job. Team members can bring experience and approaches from a range of different backgrounds. Look to your mission and objectives to determine who is needed on the team to make sure its goals can be accomplished.

All members need to know their role or assignment on the team and what they are responsible for doing. In particular, they need to know how their work will contribute to the overall work of the team. Roles need to remain flexible so that team members do not think 'that's not my job!' when others need help. Some work will be shared by all, but not everyone can do everything, and so members need roles because they need to know what they can expect from each other. Without clarity, no one will be able to feel a valuable and valued member of the team.

You may want to include catering, facilities, graphic reproduction, audio visual and IT teams within your network if you think their presence on your internal networking team will enhance your working abilities and productivity, or may at least want to invite them to some of your regular meetings so you can all understand each other and know what is required of each other.

Once you know who should be on the team, you need to look at what each person will do to support the team in its mission. The best way to go about this is to list each team member and define the roles and responsibilities of each. This will help you:

- match team members to roles;
- spot gaps in skills and abilities that are necessary for the team to reach its goals;
- decide who will be the team leader;
- decide who is the liaison spokesperson between the team and the other stakeholders (ie a 'champion');
- determine who is responsible for what duties and outcomes.

Example:

The team will be made up of all assistants in the organization plus a 'champion' from the senior executive team, a member of the facilities department, catering department, information technology, graphics department and the audio-visual department.

You may also want to appoint specialist roles using the expertise and experience of certain assistants to whom others can go for help: for example, an expert on Excel, PowerPoint or social media – even bilingual speakers etc.

Example of role description for team leader:

[Name of leader] will take the role of Team Leader in which she/he will be responsible for:

- *ensuring this Team Charter is followed and kept up to date;*
- *managing the day-to-day operations of the team and the team's deliverables;*
- *managing people conflict;*
- *providing support and assistance to individual team members;*
- *providing updates for the company intranet.*

Authority and empowerment

With the roles defined, you now need to look at what team members can and can't do to achieve the mission. For example, in what capacity are team members allowed to use social media and for how long? What is within the team's remit and what actions require approval? How should team members resolve any conflicts between their day jobs and the team mission?

Resources and support available

This section lists the resources available to the team to accomplish its goals. Whether lunch will be provided for face-to-face team meetings, budgets, time allocated for meetings and for carrying out 'expert' roles, equipment and people. In conjunction with the performance assessments, changes to the resources required should be monitored regularly.

As well as this, it should detail the training and coaching support available to the team.

Operations

This section outlines how the team will operate on a day-to-day basis. This can be as detailed or as minimal as appropriate.

Example: Team meetings

- *The first team meeting will be on 28 February... at 2.00 pm.*
- *The team will meet every month during lunch time, 12.30 pm to 13.30 pm, and lunch will be included.*
- *Every other month will be a lunch-and-learn session with a different trainer – topics to be discussed and decided by the whole team. This will last 1.5 hours.*
- *Each member is expected to update the team on any new findings or suggestions that can help the team work better together.*
- *If a member is unable to attend, a notification must be sent to the team leader and someone else designated to report on the status and communicate further expectations.*
- *A summary of each meeting will be prepared by the 'minute-taker' and posted on the intranet two days later.*

Seven ground rules for effective teamwork

The following guidelines will help you set fair and reasonable team rules and you should customize the ground rules to fit the needs and mission of your team:

- **Respect**: Make it clear that team members should remain polite, attentive and respectful at all times, with unconditional respect for everyone.

- **Admit to mistakes and learn from them**: Team members should not lay blame on anyone else. If they make a mistake they should admit to it and learn from it. This will help to create a supportive, non-threatening environment that's conducive to effective relationships and teamwork.

- **Be productive at all times**: As the team leader, make it clear to everyone that they must be on time for work in the morning and back from lunch. They should try and keep procrastination to the minimum and keep on track with the goals, aims and mission of the team. No team member should shirk their responsibilities and all should be accountable.

- **Actively listen to each other**: The team should listen to each other, not only to their words but also to their body language and congruence. Understand what is meant and not just what is said.

- **Confidentiality**: Team members should be confidential at all times and avoid gossiping, helping to keep office politics to a minimum.

- **Make everyone feel equal and included**: No one should feel alienated and everyone should feel the support and friendship of each other. Team members should be able to freely interact, understand and respect each others' differences and debate ideas with openness. Everyone's contribution should be taken into consideration and appreciated. If you have a team lunch meeting remember to invite everyone.

- **Deal with conflict**: Conflict should be dealt with by nipping it in the bud and not by waiting for it to escalate. Be open and honest, act like 'adult to adult', look for win–win solutions and clear the air, making way for a productive working environment.

Negotiation and agreement/sign off

A good Team Charter emerges naturally through a process of negotiation. The team and its boss(es)' 'clients' establishes the context and mission. Objectives, composition, roles, boundaries and resources ideally emerge through negotiation between the champion, the team leader, the team and other stakeholders.

Five keys to success when creating a Team Charter:

- Discuss within the team and with the team leader to make sure that the mission and Team Charter is credible.

- Have assertive negotiation with the 'Champion' and the team leader to ensure that the mission is achievable, and that sufficient resources and budget (if appropriate) are available.

- Ensure discussion amongst all members and stakeholders to make sure the team has the relevant support in terms of development, feedback and training.

- All members and stakeholders need to approve the Team Charter and sign it off. This helps everyone to commit fully to the mission, objectives, principles, roles and responsibilities and then hold each other accountable.

- Continually evaluate, enhance, improve and develop the Team Charter with change of procedures, rules and processes.

Belbin® team roles

Importance of team balance

The management writer Jim Collins talks about team building in terms of 'getting the right people on the bus'. Collins argues that while it is the leader's role to decide where the bus is going and how it's going to get there, there's little point in setting out until the right people are on the bus, in the right seats.

When a team is being formed, it is advisable to employ a variety of team styles to ensure a balanced team profile. Successful sports teams make sure that the right person is playing the correct position. In a football team, for example, not having enough forwards who can score the goals will make it very hard for that team to win. The same principle applies in a work team.

Too many of one behavioural style will create gaps in other areas of the team.

The ideal team will have a balance of all the team styles that make up a winning team. However, in the real world most teams do not have a complete set of roles. It is important to recognize where the gaps are and try to ensure someone fulfils the role.

Most people have a number of 'preferred team roles' or behaviours they frequently and naturally display. We also have 'manageable roles', or secondary roles that might not be the most natural course of behaviour for us, but that we can assume if required and that we might wish to cultivate. We can take these roles when there is a gap in the team or where there may only be four or five in a team and so members need to double up on their behavioural styles in order for the team to be the most effective it can be.

We also have least preferred roles, those we should not assume since we'll be playing against type. In this instance, the effort is likely to be great, and the outcome poor. If work requires team roles other than our own, it is a much better bet to find and work with others who possess roles complementary to our own. The Belbin® philosophy is about celebrating and making the most of individual differences. By identifying our team roles, we can ensure that we use our strengths to advantage and that we manage our weaknesses as best we can. Sometimes, this means being aware of the pitfalls and making an effort to avoid them.

Belbin® team roles explained (with the kind permission of BELBIN® www.belbin.com)

In the 1970s, Dr Meredith Belbin and his research team at Henley Management College set about observing teams, with a view to finding out where and how these differences come about. They wanted to control the dynamics of teams to discover if and how problems could be pre-empted and avoided.

Dr Meredith Belbin has defined nine team roles:

Action-oriented roles:	Shaper, Implementer, Completer-Finisher.
People-oriented roles:	Coordinator, Teamworker, Resource Investigator.
Thinking-oriented roles:	Plant, Monitor-Evaluator, Specialist.

As well as the strength or contribution that each role provides, each 'team role' was also found to have an 'allowable weakness' that is the flipside of the behavioural characteristics. This is allowable in the team because of the strength that goes with it.

Shaper (SH)

Characteristics: Shapers are highly motivated people with a lot of nervous energy and a great need for achievement. They are honest, straightforward and open with others. Usually they are aggressive extroverts and possess strong drive and are challenging, dynamic and thrive on pressure. SHs like to challenge others and their concern is to win. They like to lead and to push others into action. If obstacles arise, they will find a way round. Headstrong and assertive, they tend to show strong emotional response to any form of disappointment or frustration. They make sure the team is achieving goals.

SHs are thick skinned and argumentative and may lack interpersonal understanding. This is the most competitive team role.

Function: SHs generally make good managers because they get things moving, generate action and thrive under pressure. They are excellent at sparking life into a team and are very useful in groups where political complications are apt to slow things down.

Allowable weakness: Prone to frustration and irritation. Could risk becoming aggressive and bad-humoured in their attempts to get things done. Offend people's feelings.

Disallowable weakness: Inability to recover a situation with good humour or apology.

Implementer (IMP)

Characteristics: Implementers have practical common sense and a good deal of self-control and discipline.

They favour hard work and tackle problems in a systematic fashion. On a wider front the IMP is typically a person whose loyalty and interest lie with the company/team/boss and who is less concerned with the pursuit of self-interest. IMPs may lack spontaneity and show signs of rigidity. They are reliable and efficient and can turn ideas into practical actions. They organize systems and ensure everyone follows the laid out procedures.

Function: IMPs are useful to an organization because of their reliability and capacity for application. They succeed because they are efficient and because they have a sense of what is feasible and relevant.

Allowable weakness: Adherence to the orthodox and proven. Somewhat inflexible. Slow to respond to new possibilities.

Disallowable weakness: Obstructing change – might be slow to relinquish their plans in favour of positive changes.

Completer-Finisher (CF)

Characteristics: Completer-Finishers have a great capacity for follow-through and attention to detail.

They are conscientious, search out errors and omissions, and polish and perfect whatever they are working on.

They try to raise standards in all they do and promote excellence. They are unlikely to start anything that they cannot finish. They are motivated by internal anxiety, yet outwardly they may appear unruffled. Typically, they are introverted and require little in the way of external stimulus or incentive. CFs can be intolerant of those with a casual disposition. They are not often keen on delegating, preferring to tackle all tasks themselves.

Function: CFs are invaluable where tasks demand close concentration and a high degree of accuracy. They foster a sense of urgency within a team and are good at meeting schedules. In management they excel by the high standard to which they aspire and by their concern for precision, attention to detail and follow-through.

Allowable weakness: Perfectionism. Inclined to worry unduly. They can split hairs on trivial issues.

Disallowable weakness: They can allow perfectionism to turn into obsessive behaviour, becoming over protective of the boundaries of their job area.

Coordinator (CO)

Characteristics: The distinguishing feature of Coordinators is their ability to clarify goals, promote decision making and encourage others to work towards shared goals. They establish an air of authority over the team with a mature approach as they are trusting, confident and they delegate readily. In interpersonal relations they are quick to spot individual talents and to use them in the pursuit of team objectives. COs have a broad and worldly outlook and generally command respect. They bring others into discussions when they have things to contribute and hold the group together. They give praise and encourage others.

Function: COs are well placed when put in charge of a team of people with diverse skills and personal characteristics. They perform better in dealing with colleagues of near or equal rank than in directing junior subordinates. Their motto might well be 'consultation with control' and they usually believe in tackling problems calmly. In some teams COs are inclined to clash with Shapers due to their contrasting management styles.

Allowable weakness: Inclination to be lazy if someone else can be found to do the work. Can be seen as manipulative. Can offload personal work. Might over-delegate, leaving themselves little work to do.

Disallowable weakness: Taking credit for the effort of the team.

Teamworker (TW)

Characteristics: Teamworkers are the most supportive members of a team. They are cooperative, perceptive, diplomatic, sociable and concerned about others. They have a great capacity for flexibility and adapting to different situations and people. They are good listeners and are generally popular members of a team. They promote a good team atmosphere by reacting to the needs of others. They support members of the team when necessary. They become brokers in times of argument and defuse any hostility. They operate with sensitivity.

Function: The role of the TW is to prevent interpersonal problems arising within a team and thus allow all team members to contribute effectively. Not liking friction, they will go to great lengths to avoid it. It is not uncommon for TWs to become senior managers, especially if Shapers dominate divisional management positions. This creates a climate in which the diplomatic and perceptive skills of a TW become real assets, particularly under a managerial regime where conflicts are liable to arise or to be artificially suppressed. TW managers are seen as a threat to no one and are therefore the most accepted and favoured people to serve under. TWs have a lubricating effect on teams. Morale is improved and people seem to cooperate better when they are around.

Allowable weakness: Indecision on crucial issues and might become indecisive when unpopular decisions need to be made.

Disallowable weakness: Avoid situations that may entail pressure.

Resource Investigator (RI)

Characteristics: Resource Investigators are often enthusiastic, quick-off-the-mark extroverts. They are good at communicating with people both inside and outside the company. They are natural negotiators and are adept at exploring new opportunities and developing contacts. Although not a great source of original ideas, the RI is effective when it comes to picking up other people's ideas and developing them, so they would develop the ideas of the 'Plant'. As the name suggests, they are skilled at finding out what is available and what can be done. They usually receive a warm reception from others because of their own outgoing nature.

RIs have relaxed personalities with a strong inquisitive sense and a readiness to see the possibilities in anything new. However, unless they remain stimulated by others, their enthusiasm rapidly fades.

Function: RIs are good at exploring and reporting back on ideas, developments or resources outside the team. They are the best people to set up external contacts and to carry out any subsequent negotiations. They also have an ability to think on their feet and to probe others for information.

Allowable weakness: Loss of enthusiasm once initial excitement has passed. Talk too much so others cannot get enough air time.

Disallowable weakness: Letting clients down by neglecting to follow up.

Plant (PL)

Characteristics: Plants are innovators and inventors and can be highly creative. They can create an original piece of work and invent a new way of tackling the issues in hand. They provide the seeds and ideas from which major developments spring. Usually they prefer to operate by themselves at some distance from other members of the team, using their imagination and often working in an unorthodox manner. They tend to be introverted and react strongly to criticism and praise. Their ideas may often be radical and may lack practical constraint.

They are independent, clever and original and may be weak in communicating with other people on a different wave length.

Function: The main function of a plant is to generate new proposals, ideas and suggestions, and to solve complex problems and work out solutions. Plants are often needed in the initial stages of a project or when a project is failing to progress. Too many plants in one team may be counterproductive as they tend to spend their time reinforcing their own ideas and engaging each other in combat.

Evaluate your own ideas. Look at things from a different angle.

Allowable weakness: Could be unorthodox or forgetful and neglect practical matters. Ignore incidentals. Too pre-occupied to communicate effectively.

Disallowable weakness: Claim ownership of ideas when cooperation would yield better results.

Monitor-Evaluator (ME)

Characteristics: Monitor-Evaluators are serious-minded, cautious individuals with a built-in immunity from being overenthusiastic. They are slow in making decisions, preferring to think things over. Usually they have a high critical thinking ability. They have a capacity for shrewd judgements that take all factors into consideration. A good ME is seldom wrong. They are strategic and perceptive and see all options. They judge accurately and provide a balanced opinion on all ideas and options. They can dampen the positive approach of the team.

Function: MEs are best suited to analysing problems and evaluating ideas and suggestions. They are very good at weighing up the pros and cons of options. To many outsiders the ME may appear as dry, boring or even overcritical. Some people are surprised that they become managers. Nevertheless, many MEs occupy strategic posts and thrive in high-level appointments. In some jobs, success or failure hinges on a relatively small number of crunch decisions. This is ideal territory for an ME; for the person who is never wrong is the one who scores in the end.

Allowable weakness: Scepticism with logic (ie somebody who doubts something is true).

Disallowable weakness: Cynicism without logic (ie somebody who believes that others actions are insincere). Could be overly critical and slow moving.

Specialist (SP)

Characteristics: Specialists are dedicated individuals who pride themselves on acquiring technical skills and specialized knowledge. Their priorities centre on maintaining professional standards and on furthering and defending their own field. While they show great pride in their own subject, they usually lack interest in other areas. Eventually the SP becomes the expert by sheer commitment. There are few people who have either the single-mindedness or the aptitude to become a first-class SP. They cultivate a sense of professionalism and encourage fellow team members to trust their knowledge. They need to keep their expertise and skills up to date. They provide knowledge and skills in rare supply.

Function: SPs have an indispensable part to play in some teams, for they provide the rare skills upon which the organization's service or product is based. As managers, they command support because they know more about their subject than anyone else and can usually be called upon to make decisions based on in-depth experience.

Allowable weakness: Acquiring knowledge for its own sake. May have a tendency to focus narrowly on their own subject of choice.

Disallowable weakness: Ignoring factors outside own area of competence.

By identifying our own 'team role', we can ensure that we use our strengths to advantage and that we manage our weaknesses the best we can. Sometimes, this means being aware of the pitfalls and making an effort to avoid them.

A person's overall strongest roles are the ones most appreciated by other people. When you know your strongest team role, you should develop and play the role with enthusiasm because this is where you are likely to raise your profile. However you should remember to play down the allowable weakness of that role and also to try and eliminate the non-allowable weakness.

One way of arranging the nine task/preferences is as follows: two functions are concerned with leadership and setting direction (Shaper and Coordinator); two are concerned with establishing and extending ideas and external contacts (Plant and Resource-Investigator); three are concerned with aspects of the detail and quality of the internal working of the team and its performance and products (Completer-Finisher, Monitor-Evaluator and Teamworker); one is concerned with getting that work out into the world once it is under way (Implementer), and one has a focus on the Specialist contribution of professional knowledge etc.

To achieve the best balance in a team there should be:

- one Coordinator or Shaper (not both) as leader;
- chairperson;
- a Monitor-Evaluator to maintain honesty and clarity;
- one or more 'Plants' to stimulate ideas;
- one or more Implementers, Teamworkers, Resource investigators and Completer-Finishers to make things happen.

How Belbin® and TetraMap® behavioural styles work together in the stages of team development

Belbin®'s team roles can be mapped against the TetraMap® behavioural styles. TetraMap is a registered trademark of TetraMap International in New Zealand, UK and other countries. The following content is the author's interpretation of TetraMap® and is reproduced with permission from TetraMap International. See Chapter 7 on 'How to communicate with different personality and behavioural styles'.

In the 'Forming' stage, the type of behaviours shown by those needing to act, who like a challenge and are not afraid of taking risks (for example TetraMap®'s 'Fire' and Belbin®'s 'Plant') may jump into action enjoying the excitement and novelty of exploring something new. There are others who need specific information, full details and time to plan schedules (TetraMap®'s 'Air' – Belbin®'s 'Completer-Finisher'), may not be able to do anything straight away and are more likely to wait for the information they need to take matters forward.

The 'Storming' stage will last for a longer or shorter time depending on personalities and behavioural styles within the team and also of course on whether the people involved have the knowledge and willingness to use the information in this chapter! The Water Elements and Teamworkers will be trying to get everyone working alongside each other and helping each other making sure everyone is included.

The 'Norming' phase is when deadlines are looming and a sense of urgency is created for action to be taken. The need for action is the key as it unfreezes those held in place by a 'need to know before acting' (TetraMap®'s 'Earth' and Belbin®'s 'Monitor-Evaluator').

It's during the 'Norming' stage that productivity starts to rise and the teams start to perform well together. The Performing stage is when the team's focus will be entirely on how best to work and share knowledge together to achieve the best possible results. Individual and team profiles should be shared so that everyone understands how everyone fits into the team and which of your strengths come into play and when.

Summary

As a team leader you need to understand the different roles that make up a team as well as be aware of the different behavioural styles of team members. Understanding the five different stages that a team inevitably goes through and what you can do as team leader to help that process progress smoothly can be the make or break of an effective team. Using the Team Charter, including guidelines for effective teamwork, should enable you to keep control of the dynamics of the team so that it can be the most effective and productive and conducive for a fun and exciting place to work.

Performance management

05

This chapter is about managing the performance of ourselves and others; it explains the process and procedures for recruiting, from attracting people to appraising them. It defines the role or job analysis of a 'professional assistant': what the characteristics, attitude, skills and behaviours are of the 'professional assistant' and it includes a resource with a sample 'person specification' that you can use to recruit or check your skills etc against.

The chapter also includes tips on CV writing, applying for jobs and interview techniques both from the recruiter and potential candidate's point of view.

There are tips on making inductions worthwhile and memorable by using a structured induction programme so that you can help new recruits feel a part of the organization from the very beginning. It will explain how to create a 'standard operating procedures' binder and a work schedule for reference so anyone can step into your job if you are unexpectedly absent or plan to be away from work.

It discusses the need for performance management and how to conduct appraisals, including tips for the appraiser and the appraisee.

Performance management

Performance management is a strategic process that covers the whole life cycle of an employee, including recruitment, induction, engagement such as training and development, performance appraisal and promotion. It is about the assessment of performance as well as potential and it results in retaining the best and most effective workers.

Performance management is about having the right people in the right job, working with the right boss and the right team, with the right competencies, and making sure that they receive the right development tools in order to be effective (ie 'doing the right things') as well as efficient (ie 'doing things right').

Performance management is an essential ingredient for organizational success and depends on four critical factors, which are that everyone understands:

- the mission and purpose of the organization;
- the strategic goals or key result areas that will lead to organizational success;
- their individual roles and responsibilities;
- how those fit with organizational objectives.

On a strategic organizational level, the idea of performance management is to measure performance against goals that are aligned to the organization to meet current and future business objectives. On an individual basis it is about reaching your potential and, according to Maslow's hierarchical level of needs (see Chapter 2 on 'How to motivate yourself and your teams'), it is about reaching self-actualization.

The business strategy must include responsibilities for team leaders, supervisors and line managers to develop the skills of their immediate subordinates.

Recruiting

The ability to attract candidates depends upon how potential applicants view the organization, the industry or sector in which it operates and whether they share the values of that organization. The creation of an attractive employer brand is an important factor in recruiting.

Recruitment is the process of getting the right person, in the right place, at the right time and it is crucial to organizational performance. Recruitment isn't always straightforward, as people might look excellent on their resumé/ curriculum vitae (CV) but when you meet them, your heart sinks because they just don't have that hidden ingredient that's right for your company, or when you meet them in person they do not portray what was on their CV.

Also, if you are the one being recruited, your hopes may be dashed when you realize at the interview that the job or company isn't right for you no matter how much research you may have done on it. Remember the recruitment process is a two-way process – both recruiter and recruitee have to believe that they are the right fit for each other. Recruitees need to find out and research thoroughly about the business before and during the recruitment process and consider whether the organization is one they would like to work for.

A popular way to recruit is through the internet and job search engines, including the social media networking site LinkedIn. Other ways of recruiting are through internal applications, internal referral schemes, job fairs, newspaper advertising, job centres, networking, word of mouth and recommendation. No matter how the hiring is conducted it is absolutely certain that any potential employee will have a search done on them via the internet, so do be careful about what you or other people put on the social media websites about you, including pictures, if you want to be considered as a professional person and a potential new recruit. You should regularly 'Google' yourself to see what is on the web about you!

The recruitment process involves working through a series of stages:

1 Defining the role/job analysis and creating a person specification.
2 Attracting applications.
3 Managing the application and selection process.
4 Making the appointment and conducting the interview.

All those involved in recruitment activities should be equipped with the appropriate knowledge and skills. As a team leader of executive assistants I was always involved in the second interview for hiring members for my team, the first interview being the screening interview conducted either by HR or an agency. It is at the recruiting stage that first impressions and the ability to build rapport instantly are so very important. It is very important that the line manager/supervisor is involved with developing the job description and person specification as well as at the interview stage.

Job analysis

Before recruiting for a new or existing position, it is important to invest time in gathering information about the nature of the job. This means thinking not only about the content (such as the tasks) making up the job, but also the job's purpose, the outputs required by the job holder and how it fits into the organization's structure. This analysis should form the basis of a job description and person specification/job profile. However, I do not believe in keeping to 'job descriptions' to the letter – you have to be flexible and continually add to your job description where appropriate.

The job analysis leads to writing a job description. This explains the job to the candidates, and helps the recruitment process by providing a clear guide to all involved about the requirements of the job. It can also be used to communicate expectations about performance to employees and managers to help ensure effective performance in the job.

Job description

Many people ask what are the duties, roles, job description, traits, skills, behaviours of today's assistant, and the answer is: it is about being proactive and making your role whatever you want it to be, and taking on new and exciting responsibilities at every opportunity. The potential for an assistant is absolutely massive! Of course there will be key skills and duties involved but this is only the base – the rest is up to you and your tenacity to improve and evolve, and as a leader you should encourage this in others.

There is much debate around what are the differences between personal assistant, secretary, executive assistant, management assistant, admin assistant, business partner, business manager, office administrator and any other name given to the role of a 'professional assistant'. The official name given to this role varies between countries, companies, industries and departments. Individuals in different countries and companies can be doing similar roles and have different titles.

I would also like to mention here that there are also virtual assistants who work out of their homes and are often self-employed contractors who do much the same work for clients on a freelance basis. They are truly their own boss like any professional entrepreneur and may also have associates and employ people.

The skills and attitudes of the assistant are so important. Resource 2 'Person specification', which can be downloaded from **www.surefrance.com**, outlines many of the skills, behaviours and attitudes of an assistant, although it is not exhaustive. I have set them out as a 'person specification' that can be used in recruiting and encompasses every professional assistant role, skill and behaviour I can think of, so it does not represent one job role but an amalgamation of many. I have also included many of the job roles that an assistant conducts, and if you are not currently performing any of these duties and would like to – then simply ask to see if you can get involved in these areas; remember 'if you don't ask, you don't get'.

Person specification

A person specification is written by the organization and outlines the type of person they want in order to match the right person to the job. It states the 'essential' and 'desirable' criteria to determine which competencies are absolutely necessary for the job and which would be 'good to have', to help with selection purposes. By using Resource 2 mentioned above, you can find a list of competencies used in the variable assistant role.

In addition, the person specification might include some or all of the following:

- educational qualifications;
- previous experience required; for example, how many years in the role as an assistant to a CEO etc;
- specialized skills; for example, ability to supervise/manage others, ability to manage projects etc;
- aptitudes; for example, verbal reasoning, numerical aptitude;
- interests; for example, social activities, sporting activities and hobbies;
- personal circumstances; for example, ability to work shifts, full or part time;
- memberships; for example, member of a PA network, member of a Professional Institute etc.

Person specifications have to be prepared and used with great care. In particular, it is important to ensure that the list of essential or desired competencies does not lead to unlawful discrimination against potential employees. For example, in the UK we cannot discriminate against sex, age and disability.

Application forms

There are two main formats in which applications are likely to be received: the resumé/curriculum vitae (CV) or the application form, which can be submitted either on paper or electronically via the internet or e-mail.

Application forms allow for information to be presented in a consistent format, and therefore make it easier to collect information from job applicants in a systematic way and assess objectively the candidate's suitability for the job.

CVs

The advantage of CVs is that they give candidates the opportunity to sell themselves in their own way and don't restrict the fitting of information into boxes, which often happens on application forms. However, CVs make it possible for candidates to include lots of additional, irrelevant material that may make them harder to assess consistently. They should be no more than two pages long and typed up logically and attractively.

All applications should be treated confidentially and circulated only to those individuals involved in the recruitment process. All solicited applications (such as responses to advertisements) should also be acknowledged, and where possible so should all unsolicited applications. Prompt acknowledgment is good practice and presents a positive image of the organization.

CVs should be tailored to the industry and to the job applied for, and therefore sending what is obviously a generic CV does not show initiative or keenness. Examples of achievements are important signals of the business acumen, skills and attitudes of the applicant.

Automated scanning programs

Many companies use automated scanners to sieve through the CVs and could potentially miss suitable candidates simply because they did not use the words the scanner looks for. However, be aware also that some applicants write the words that the scanner looks for in white on the paper (so it cannot be seen by the naked eye). These words match the words in the job advertisement so that scanners will pick out their CV. Therefore the scanner may pick out CVs of people who may not be suitable candidates but who have simply put the right words on their application.

When screening CVs and preparing questions for the interview, look for achievements and accomplishments that support applicants' claims about their behaviour, attitude, skills and personality and question them about these. For example look for statements and verbs that show their achievements such as: created, came in under-budget; increased; reduced; improved; developed, accomplished; researched; won and awards. Look for evidence – for example if they say they are motivated, a team player, outstanding, effective – what proves this? Also check for quotes from their leaders, supervisors that back up their claims to be excellent team leaders etc. Look to see if they have received any appropriate awards or any other forms of recognition.

Interviews

It is important for both interviewer and interviewee to have excellent communication skills and to be able to build rapport easily and quickly. Remember when reading body language that you can only read it well when you know someone really well and that you should take at least four or five different clues to really know what people are thinking.

The invitation letter should tell candidates that they should advise the organization in advance of any particular arrangements that need to be made to accommodate them on arrival or during the interview; for instance, ramp access.

Interview preparation

Structured interviews

Interviews should be structured so that questions are planned carefully before the interview to suit the attributes and behaviours required for the job and to ensure that all candidates for the same job are asked the same questions so you can have a fair and comparable assessment of each candidate.

Screening interviews

The screening interview could be done by Human Resources or the agency, which will sift through all the applications and choose the candidates that best match the person specification. They may even do typing and software packaging tests at this stage as there is no point in putting someone forward for a second interview if they cannot match basic requirements. Telephone interviews may also be the first interview to help screen applicants.

Second interview

You should conduct the second interview and you may have the authority to hire or you may wish to bring back, for example, three suitable candidates for third interview for the assistant to meet with the manager(s) they will work with. These will be the candidates who have the right credentials, ethos and tenacity, and are suitable to fit in with the existing team of assistants and suit the personalities of the managers they would work for. When it reaches the third stage it is more about the 'personality fit' and whether they would work well with the manager.

You may want to have someone else with you in the second interview who will work closely with the candidate to make sure they are both happy to work with each other.

Before the meeting, read through the candidate's CV again and make notes where you want to clarify any points, together with the pre-prepared list of questions that you need to ask.

Location of interview

Choose a quiet conference room where you will not be disturbed by people or phones, and if possible, position the chairs so there is no table between you (acting as a barrier) and put your chairs at 45° angles to each other so you are not facing each other directly. Remember you can influence people better when you are on the right-hand side of them.

The interview

Ensure that you have the applicant's CV (with your notes) and covering letter to hand as well as a copy of the job description and person specification. Not only will they be useful for reference but they will also demonstrate to the candidate that you are fully prepared.

As the candidate, you should be a few minutes early and treat everyone with respect and dignity, be confident and keep eye contact, actively listen carefully to the questions and answer the question asked, although you should also expand on your answer where appropriate.

Bear in mind the following tips:

- As the interviewer, you should welcome the candidate with a warm, friendly handshake and smile using eye contact. Introduce yourself and any other interviewers. Begin each interview with an informal chat to help interviewees settle down. This will help to put the candidates at ease as they will always be nervous. Explain what format the interview will take and how long it will last, and whether any travel expenses will be reimbursed and how they will receive their expenses.

- Ask the candidate if it is okay to take notes during the interview as a matter of politeness. Just as they will not remember everything, neither will you! If you are conducting several interviews in succession, give yourself time to write further notes about the interview and your thoughts on the candidate, including your gut reaction, as it will be hard to review the results of the interview at a later stage without them.

- If the candidate asks to take notes either on a notepad or iPad etc, then realize that this is an initiative that the assistant will use within their role and is a plus point when discussing the successful candidate.

- This is an opportunity to describe the job and the responsibilities in more detail; assess the candidate's ability to perform in the role; discuss with the candidate details such as start dates, holidays, training provisions, and terms and conditions such as employee benefits.

- Give a brief overview of the company, the department and the role on offer. It is important to always give a positive impression of the company to the candidate as a 'good employer' because you should always take opportunities to enhance the brand of the company and you never know where they may end up working – it could be a client of your company. Even if you don't want to give them a job, you should still encourage them to think that they really want the job because it's a great place to work and they leave with a good impression of the company.

- Give plenty of 'talk time' to interviewees otherwise you will not find out enough about them. A huge mistake that interviewers make is that they talk too much and then wonder how they hired the wrong person for the job!

- Ask the candidates about themselves, being careful about how you phrase your questions (see more information on types of questions in Chapter 9, and remember to download Resource 3, 'Example questions for recruiting'. The Resource can also be used by potential candidates to help them prepare for an interview.) You may need to consider relevant legislation when interviewing; for example, in the UK you are not allowed to ask for some personal information such as potentially discriminatory questions like: 'Are you planning to have children in the next few years?' Don't ask too many 'closed' questions but do ask open-ended questions that encourage the candidate to speak freely and remember to avoid leading questions.

  The interview questions need to give you a clear indication of not only the candidate's technical abilities but also their personality.

The aim of the questions should be to answer the following question 'Will this person fit into the business from a work and personality point of view and help to increase company profits?'

- Take candidates chronologically through their CVs (which they should know off by heart so there is no need to give them a copy) and take a quick tour of the candidate's roles from past to present. You should ask competency-based and behavioural questions relevant to the role. Pick out the key skills the candidate will need for the role – for example, creativity, leadership, resilience, time management – and ask questions around these attributes.

   As well as asking questions you can also give the candidate a statement and then ask him or her to expand – for example 'You have had a lot of experience in managing teams. Tell me about it' – and be prepared to probe further.

- Remember to have fun. It is okay to use humour – it will put the candidate at ease. Do watch the time. I would give each candidate a maximum of an hour so that you can really get to know each other and to give a real chance to match and mirror, pace and lead as well as giving them time to ask questions. However if you know that the candidate is not suitable you can cut this time short (in a way that still leaves them with a positive impression of the company). You will find with the candidates you like and think are suitable, the hour will fly by and the conversation will be flowing and the opposite is true with candidates who are not suitable.

When interviewing make sure you do not fall into the trap of making the following mistakes (summarized by Anderson and Shackleton):

- **The self-fulfilling prophecy effect**: Interviewers may ask questions designed to confirm initial impressions gained either before the interview or in its early stages.

- **The stereotyping effect**: Interviewers sometimes assume that particular characteristics are typical of members of a particular group.

- **The halo and horns effect**: A tendency to allow your judgement of the interviewee to be unduly influenced by an unfavourable (horns) or favourable (halo) first impression based on appearances.

- **The contrast effect**: Interviewers can allow the experience of interviewing one candidate to affect the way they interview others who are seen later in the selection process.

- **The similar-to-me effect**: Interviewers sometimes subconsciously give preference to candidates they perceive as having a similar background, career history, personality or attitudes to themselves.
- **The personal liking effect**: Interviewers may make decisions on the basis of whether they personally like or dislike the candidate.
- **The temporal effect**: Assuming that a candidate's behaviour at the interview, for example nervous, is typical of their general disposition.
- **The expectancy effect**: Giving undue influence to positive or negative expectations of a candidate formed from the CV or application form.
- **The primacy effect**: Putting too much emphasis on impressions gained and information assimilated early in the interview.
- **Negative information bias effect**: Giving more weight to perceived negative points about candidates than to those that are most positive.

You have to conduct structured interviews carefully so that they do not seem too rigid, and you have to be flexible because you will need to use probing questions depending on their answers, but at the same time each interview for the same job has to be comparable.

You may also use assessment centres, psychological and psychometric testing, 'in-tray' exercises, role-plays, giving a presentation, numeracy tests etc.

Closing the interview

It may be appropriate to ask what notice period the interviewee has to give. However, it is not advisable to offer candidates positions at the end of an interview or even let them know that they will be asked back for a third interview, because you need time to compare the different interviews and reflect on your thoughts and possibly discuss them with the first interviewer and your co-interviewer (if you had one). Let them know that they will be contacted in the next few days (and make sure you do this even for those who will not be asked back).

An informal chat often helps to end on a friendly note. Make sure that you have covered all your points and the candidates have covered theirs. If the candidate has travelled a fair distance, this may be an opportunity to offer them reimbursement for their expenses. Your closing actions will have an impression on the candidate and it is important to make sure that they reflect well on both you and your company.

At the third interview, as well as the candidate having a 20–30 minute interview with the manager(s), it will be useful both for the candidates and the wider team to meet each other. It would also be good for the candidates to see the environment in which they would be working. Gaining the commitment of the immediate manager/supervisor by involving them in the selection process is vital to ensuring that the new employee is settled successfully into the organization.

Reviews and selecting the best candidate(s)

The review is a chance for you to reflect on the interviews. If you conducted the interviews with a colleague, it is a chance to compare notes and discuss individual candidate performances. If the candidate has come back for a third interview with the manager(s), then you should all be involved in discussing the three candidates to find the most suitable one for the job. Sometimes managers need persuading and influencing if you firmly believe that one of the candidates is highly suitable, and you need to give reasons and examples. Be objective in your decisions. Remember the question you really need answering is: 'Will this person fit into the business from a work and personality point of view and help to increase company profits?'

Try to send each candidate a thank you letter/e-mail/phone call as soon as possible for attending the interview and inform them of your decision. Most active job seekers will be making arrangements for and attending interviews for several different jobs so it is important not to allow too much time to pass between interviews, especially if you are keen to have them back.

For the candidate: It is good practice and good manners to write a letter of thanks for inviting you to the interview and this letter may even sway the interviewer to ask you back for the next stage!

References

A recruitment policy should state clearly how references will be used, when in the recruitment process they will be taken up and what kind of references will be necessary (for example, from current and former employers and personal character references). These rules should be applied consistently. Candidates should always be informed of the procedure for taking up references. References are most frequently asked for after the applicant has been given a 'provisional offer'.

The purpose of references is to obtain information about a candidate's employment history, qualifications, experience and/or an assessment of the candidate's suitability for the post in question. Prospective employers may seek information on matters including length of employment, job title, brief details of responsibilities, abilities, overall performance, time-keeping and reason for leaving.

As well as taking references employers need to carry out other pre-employment checks – particularly, for example, if the job involves working with children or vulnerable adults.

Most companies will request references to be submitted in writing, either in the form of an 'open' unstructured letter or by use of a standard form. Requesting written references provides referees with more time to reflect on the questions and the wording of answers. It is important that any reference request is marked 'private and confidential' for the attention of the named referee.

Case law has resulted in a cautious approach from people giving references. All data given in a reference should be based on fact or capable of independent verification. As a guide, references should be fair, accurate and not give a misleading overall impression of the employee.

Medical examinations

Any particular physical or medical requirement should be made clear in the job advertisement or other recruitment literature. There will be different rules and laws in each country regarding medicals; for example in the UK, The Equality Act 2010 makes it unlawful to ask candidates to complete a medical questionnaire before being offered a job. Only essential medical issues should be discussed at this stage, such as requiring specialist equipment etc.

Employment offer

The selection processes should be based on a candidate's ability to do the job, ability to make a contribution to the organization's effectiveness and their potential for development.

Offers of employment should always be made in writing. But it is important to be aware that a verbal offer of employment made in an interview is as legally binding as a letter in the UK and possibly other countries. The recruitment process should be documented accurately, with access limited to recruitment staff as there are data protection issues. Unsuccessful candidates should be notified promptly in writing and if possible given feedback, including any psychometric test results.

If you have applied for a job and have not received any feedback then ask for it so you can possibly learn from it.

Induction programme and standard operating procedures (SOP)

You should have a structured induction programme in place that should be creative, engaging and fun, and do the job of reinforcing for people that they made the right choice. Make people feel warm and welcome from the first few seconds – remember first impressions are made in seconds and take weeks or months to change, so make the right first impression of both yourself and the organization.

Create an interesting standard operating procedure (SOP) binder that will have in it everything new recruits will require to enable them to do the job effectively, including a contents page so they can easily find what they need.

You can include standard organizational procedures: for example, how to claim expenses, all relevant telephone numbers for ordering stationery, how to request IT help, information on how to order audiovisual equipment, stationery and catering, and the policies and procedures on how to book travel, as well as everything an assistant will need in your organization to help them do their job effectively.

You could include actual copies of forms required to do the job or screen prints of intranet instruction etc. The disaster recovery programme may also be included as well as a list of the official 'First-aiders' for the office and where they sit and their telephone numbers.

Include downloadable appendices from this book as well as from *The Definitive Personal Assistant & Secretarial Handbook*, 2nd edition, for example Appendix 4 'Proforma for goal setting' and Appendix 11 on 'Event management'.

Make sure it is available in electronic as well as print format.

Highly confidential information should not be contained within the SOP but must be kept safe under lock and key and this includes information such as passwords and bank details etc.

The induction programme should include people sitting with the new recruit to go through different procedures so that they are not left simply to read the SOP for themselves. The SOP is there for reference later. The more people included in the induction the better so the recruit meets different people on a more personal basis and knows who are the 'experts' in each area. Below are some action points:

Put some thought and effort into trying to make recruits feel welcome and take them around for formal introductions to the different people and departments that they will be interacting with. You could perhaps hold a complimentary lunch for them to introduce them to their work colleagues/ peers in a social setting. Remember that people can only retain so much information in one go. It may be worth spreading out the induction period over a week or two so they can digest it piece by piece. They of course should have their notepads with them at all times and writing everything down that they feel they need to remember (unless it is already in the SOP).

Having an assigned 'buddy' is really useful especially when they are doing a similar role and sit close to each other. It is also useful for the buddy to practise coaching skills and it is a way of making people's jobs more interesting and another useful addition for their CV (resumé).

Make sure recruits understand the ethos and style of the company; to help them feel that they made the right decision and to help them settle in quickly and efficiently so that they start their new job committed, engaged and productive.

Most people start a new job excited and filled with anticipation and also have a natural feeling of anxiety about what's in store for them. Let them know what the company expects of them and find out what their expectations are. Be flexible, have fun and instil loyalty from the beginning because a great induction experience actually helps with staff retention. Your aim is for recruits to begin their jobs feeling reassured, well-informed and therefore fully operational quickly and truly feeling part of an organization that they can believe in, then any difficulties that may arise later on are far easier to deal with.

Work schedule

Once new recruits are settled into the role they can create a document containing the procedures and processes that they perform (which will be much more detailed than your official job description and different from the SOP in that it will be personalized to their particular role working with individual managers). The 'work schedule' could be kept in the SOP binder and may even be inherited from the previous employee, although if you are starting in a new role you should make the position your own, and in some cases change some procedures with the agreement of your manager. The best way to create a work schedule is to track your work as you do it; this will be on an ongoing basis so you will need to update it often to begin with.

It should include exactly what you do on a daily, weekly and yearly basis so that if you are not in the office for any reason, especially if it is an unexpected absence, anyone could pick up your work schedule and be able to at least conduct the fundamental duties of your role to cover your absence effectively. It could include templates and forms, and screen prints to explain procedures and processes. It should include duties such as how your various bosses (if you work for more than one) prefer to receive their telephone messages, e-mails, post, how their in and out trays work, how to access their calendar/e-mails, information on recurring meetings, how you deal with reminder systems and important telephone numbers. It can include reminders for daily duties and how often you have face-to-face meetings to catch up on the day's work etc. It could also include duties in your role as minute taker, team leader, project leader and so on, and everything else to help the person standing in for you to be able to do your job effectively in your absence. No one should be 'precious' about their role, and the best proactive assistants are those who share information and have contingencies in place to make sure the office continues to run smoothly and effectively even when they are not there. It is also useful to train people up within your area who can cover for you when not there so that when you want to take annual leave or attend conferences and training courses, there will be no problem and nothing to stop you.

A work schedule is also useful to let your boss(es) know exactly what you do especially when it comes round to appraisal time. You may even want to ask your boss(es) whether there is anything that they would like to see in either the work schedule or the SOP and they may even use it as a reference themselves.

The work schedule and the SOP are always work-in-progress being continually updated with new information. They are for you to use as much as for those who cover you to use, particularly for the things that you do not do regularly as they act as a reference, and checklists will be key to make sure all procedures are followed correctly.

Performance management

Performance management should be strategic and integrated – it should link various aspects of the business, people management, individuals and teams.

Performance management should incorporate:

- **Performance improvement**: throughout the organization, in respect of individual, team and organizational effectiveness.

- **Development**: unless there is continuous development of individuals and teams, performance will not improve.

- **Managing behaviour**: ensuring that individuals are encouraged to behave in a way that allows and fosters better working relationships.

It is also about ensuring that managers themselves are aware of the impact of their own behaviour on the people they manage and are encouraged to identify and exhibit positive behaviours.

Performance management is about establishing a culture in which individuals and groups take responsibility for the continuous improvement of business processes and of their own skills, behaviour and contributions. It is about sharing expectations. Managers can clarify what they expect individuals and teams to do; likewise individuals and teams can communicate their expectations of how they should be managed and what they need to do their jobs. It follows that performance management is about inter-relationships and about improving the quality of all relationships and is therefore a joint process. It is also about planning – defining expectations expressed as objectives and in business plans – and about measurement. It is a continuous process operating as a continuous cycle.

Performance management should concern two major areas of measurement: performance and potential (ie what would be an employee's future performance, given the proper development skills and increased responsibility). All critical skills and learning processes should have success criteria and competencies against which employees should be measured.

When people are well managed they feel aligned, committed, on board and motivated. Their needs and wants are considered and their contributions are acknowledged. It really does help performance management if people know when there is a problem or difficulty at the time it occurs and not six months down the line at an official appraisal meeting. There should be no 'surprises' in such meetings as all problems should have been dealt with.

Day to day performance management involves dealing with people's confidence and morale and the feelings that go with that. Dealing with difficult issues requires a confidence in your own ability to handle anything that may come up.

Diagnosing poor performance

Before you can fix poor performance, you have to understand its cause. Does it come from lack of ability or low motivation? If you believe an employee is not making enough of an effort, you'll likely put increased pressure on him or her to perform. But if the real issue is ability, then increased pressure may only make the problem worse.

There are five main ways to overcome performance problems associated with a lack of ability. Consider using them in this sequence, which starts with the least intrusive:

1   **Resupply**: Check with employees that they have the right resources to do the job and verify their claim, as they will often blame external sources before admitting fault.

2   **Retrain**: Provide additional training where appropriate. Given the pace of change, especially in technology, it's easy for people skills to fall behind. Consider the many different methods of learning, including those which can be no cost, low cost. Good organizations sometimes help and encourage learning and development by offering free or subsidized college or university courses with the stipulation that people's new skills are to be used for the organization.

3   **Refit**: When the two measures above are not sufficient, consider refitting the job to the person. Are there parts of the job that can be reassigned? Analyse the individual components of the work, and try out different combinations of tasks and abilities. This may involve rearranging the jobs of other people as well. Your goal is to retain the employee, meet operational needs, and provide meaningful and rewarding work to everyone involved.

4   **Reassign**: When refitting the job doesn't turn the situation around, look at reassigning the individual. Typical job reassignments may decrease the demands of the role by reducing the need, for example, of responsibility or technical knowledge or reducing how many people they are working for. Make sure the reassigned job is still motivating, challenging and stimulating. To ensure that this strategy

is successful, demotion should never be used as punishment. It is simply that the person lacks the skills for the position or has been given too many people to work for and therefore cannot perform adequately to meet everyone's requirements.

5 **Release**: As a final option for lack of ability, you may need to let the employee go. Sometimes there are no opportunities for reassignment, and refitting isn't appropriate for the organization. In these cases, the best solution for everyone involved is for the employee to find other work. You may need to consider contractual terms and restrictions; however, in the long run, this may be the best decision for your whole team. It may well be the conclusion that the individual has come to as well.

Summary

Performance management and appraisals are strategic tools to drive learning and organizational results. There is a constant pressure to improve performance as the world is changing fast and we need to be on top of our game; competition is getting stronger and coming from new sources, both geographically and technologically.

He who stops being better stops being good.

(Oliver Cromwell)

Think about development and how performance can be improved. What new skills are needed for the future? What is required to adapt to any new situations? Is training, personal coaching or mentoring required? Seek practical, cost-effective solutions that will increase the performance and motivation of individuals and teams. Remember to read Chapter 2 on 'How to motivate yourself and your teams' and Chapter 6 on 'Coaching' to help you with performance management.

Performance problems need to be fully addressed and learning and development promoted as this creates a positive environment where people feel supported to reach their performance potential and makes everyone feel valued.

Remember to practise professional etiquette. Treat everyone with respect and dignity throughout all the processes and procedures as this is an indicator of your level of professionalism, whatever role you play.

06 Coaching

This chapter will explain coaching in detail, with a brief overview of mentoring and counselling. You will be able to enhance the working environment and your own self-esteem, and help others by providing encouragement, experience and expertise and promoting learning opportunities for colleagues. I will also explain how you can use neuro-linguistic programming tools and techniques in coaching.

As a leader, assistant, colleague, even mother, father, wife, husband, daughter or son, you will have come across many times when you wish you knew the right thing to do and say in order to help someone, whether you should say something or not and whether you should be mentoring, coaching, counselling or training somebody.

> Everyone has the capacity to change. Their ability to learn and change is rarely a function of capacity, but of choice. The coach helps the learner recognize the choices they have.

You will learn the differences between mentoring, counselling and coaching; however the crucial point is that once you have understood the benefits of each you have to decide which is right for you. To explore your reasons for wanting to help others in these areas and whether you want to take this type of commitment further, ask yourself the following questions:

- Do you want to contribute to other people's growth and success?
- Do you want to share your knowledge and experience with others?
- Do you enjoy encouraging and motivating others?
- Are you comfortable asking challenging questions?

- What type of person do you ideally want to mentor/train/coach or counsel? Can you describe the professional and personal qualities of this person? Do you want someone from the same profession or the same career path as you?
- In what areas are you willing to help? Are there any areas that you don't want to go near?
- How will helping others contribute toward your own career goals?
- How will it add to your sense of contribution and community?
- Are you prepared to invest your time on a regular basis?

Clarifying your reasons and motivations for becoming a mentor/coach/trainer and/or counsellor will help you assess your compatibility with a potential mentee/coachee.

Helping others can be a rewarding experience for you, both personally and professionally. You can improve your leadership and communication skills, learn new perspectives and ways of thinking, raise your profile, advance your career and gain a great sense of personal satisfaction.

Mentoring

Widely used in organizations, mentoring provides a mechanism by which experienced managers can pass on their wisdom – helping to shape their mentee's values and beliefs in a positive way. This is in contrast to coaching and counselling, where the emphasis is on getting people to come up with their own solutions. Mentors often give advice and guidance.

Mentoring is an essential leadership skill. In addition to managing and motivating people, it's also important that you can help others learn, grow and become more effective in their jobs.

You may not only want to be a mentor but you might also like to have a mentor yourself, so you need to know which kind of mentor you prefer. Having a mentor will also help you be a better mentor to others as you will have a better understanding of being a mentee.

Mentors help you advance in work and life, and you should be proactive and seek out people who can help you. The first step is to figure out which mentor will best meet your needs:

- The **co-mentor** can be a colleague or a friend.
- The **remote mentor** is someone outside your organization or office who can offer objective advice. You may need a remote mentor if you

are looking for a fresh perspective and you've already exhausted closer resources.

- The **distant mentor** does not even need to know s/he is your mentor! Distant mentors are people who stand out from the crowd from any walk of life. They will be someone you admire even from afar, someone with integrity and who demonstrates very specific attitudes that you wish to emulate.

Counselling

Counsellors, like coaches, create a space in which the coachees can talk about their issues. The key difference is that counselling deals primarily with helping people overcome problems whereas coaching is concerned with enhancing performance. Counselling generally tends to focus on the past in its search for reasons for why we behave the way we do. The goal is to assist people in understanding the root cause of long-standing issues. Counsellors might use 'why' questions such as 'Why do you keep doing that?' whereas coaches more often ask 'what' questions such as 'What would you like to do instead?'

In comparing coaching and counselling, the former might be seen as solution focused and action orientated, while counselling is more meaning based. Coaching addresses aspirations, objectives and tasks, while counselling focuses more on feelings. Coaching tends to be more structured while counselling can have a more free-form approach. Coaching puts greater emphasis on gaining clarity about what people want and how to achieve it, whereas counselling aims to help people to understand themselves better.

Coaching

A coach helps people to perform better than they are currently doing and develops their skills and confidence over a period of time. Coaches work in the certain belief that people have vast reserves of potential that are rarely used and that it is the coach's job to draw it out.

Whether you are a sports coach or a corporate coach the role is very similar, as coaches are committed to their individual coachees: they concentrate on improving performance without imposing limits on the performance of individuals or teams; act as a role model for others to follow; patiently work with individuals on the details of their performance; stand back and let others take the credit; and continuously learn from situations and people.

Coaching can take place informally on an ad hoc basis or formally, for example at an appraisal. You have the opportunity to coach whenever you are asked how to do something, for instance when:

- Your advice is sought by others.
- Someone tells you they can't do a particular job.
- Your opinion is asked or a decision is required.
- You see a job or task can be done in a better, cheaper or quicker way.
- Mistakes are made.

In fact in any situation where individuals are required to raise their current levels of skills, abilities and overall performance, coaching can be appropriate.

A structure for **coaching** is:

Competency:	assessing current level of performance.
Outcomes:	setting outcomes for learning.
Action:	agreeing tactics and initiating action.
CHecking:	giving feedback and making sense of what's been learnt.

Competency

When an opportunity to coach arises, avoid the quick-fix approach. The temptation is to jump in and take over and tell people what to do, but the correct way is to find out what your coachee is currently doing or has tried. In order to find a base to start coaching, you should also find out what your coachee is competent at doing. Learning this will also influence how you approach coaching and the style that you use.

What are the outcomes of coaching?

When setting outcomes, which are objectives and goals, you can create a successful picture in the minds of the coachee. To do this you can ask:

- What do you want to achieve?
- What will success look like?
- What will you see happening, hear yourself saying and feel?
- How far will it challenge and stretch you?

Action

The action stage is where coach and coachee agree on what steps are to be taken. You can initiate this by asking questions and exploring options, considering what authority people have, who can help and when the steps will take place.

Checking

As a coach you are helping your coachees to learn by giving feedback and helping them to check their progress against their outcome. If necessary you can set further stretched outcomes. The coach instils confidence in the coachee to take action. You can ask questions like:

- What did you learn?
- What might you do differently next time?
- How can you build on the good things that you did?

Remember it's never too late to coach on what happened yesterday. Use what's happening today and think about what you want your people to be doing tomorrow.

Coaching upwards

There is often a mindset that the boss knows better, but in today's fast changing world, with flatter structures and cross-functional working, this isn't always the case. Individuals need to break this mindset and view their bosses differently. They need help just as much as everybody else. To coach upwards you will need all the skills described below, and in particular: know what it is that you want to achieve and why; use your knowledge of the individual and your personal judgement of how best to approach them; make sure that they have confidence in you as a credible person and remember to choose your moment, as timing is very important.

Skills required to be an effective coach are:

- Excellent interpersonal skills in the areas of building rapport, asking questions to gain information, listening, summarizing, giving and receiving feedback, persuading, influencing and encouraging others.
- Observation skills are key for coaches as they need to be able to spot what's happening and what's not happening.
- They help people change their negative beliefs; for example believing they 'can't...' limits their ability to perform (beliefs strengthen and uphold values or what is important to people).

- They think on their feet and tackle situations creatively.
- They have empathy – seeing things from others' point of view.
- They are confident in their own abilities' and at the same time know their limits.
- They are patient and willing to make time for people.
- They have sensitivity, especially knowing when to step in and when to be quiet.
- They have a sense of humour.
- They are able to keep confidentiality.
- They must be able to show that they genuinely care about the best interests of others. The best way to radiate concern is to ask lots of questions, to engage others rather than lecture them.
- Curiosity – the best coaches are superb listeners and absorb whatever they hear. By remaining accessible, genial and supportive, such coaches motivate by offering a safe, non-judgmental sounding board.
- They help others paint a picture of a higher level of performance.
- Highly effective team facilitators and team coaches understand what drives human behaviour
- They have the ability to plan what they are going to do as far as they can.

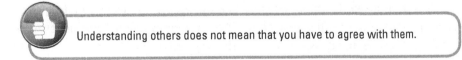

Understanding others does not mean that you have to agree with them.

Alternatives to face-to-face coaching

Face-to-face sessions are the most effective way to conduct coaching sessions, because studying body language and facial expressions are extremely important in communication. However, time available and geographical location may mean that you have to conduct some or all coaching sessions by telephone or internet phone such as video conference, e-mail correspondence or Skype. If using Skype you could use the webcam and other features as necessary. The technologies are there so put them to good use. It can help you if you have met face to face first, but it's not essential.

You may be pleasantly surprised how focused and effective telephone coaching can be.

When you cannot see the person, the key challenge is in picking up on the nuances in the absence of visual communication. Effective coaching is dependent on proper engagement and rapport, and this is a lot harder to achieve when we can't actually see the other person. More summarizing and checking understanding can counteract this. For example, when you ask a person a question that requires a degree of reflection and you are in the same room as them, you can tell whether they are actually thinking and considering their response. On the phone, you have to listen more intently for tone of voice, volume, pauses and energy in the conversation The skill is in understanding the silences – is the pause a sign that the coachee is reflecting, or is s/he struggling? You will begin to understand these types of things the more you coach over the phone. You should give particular attention to the words you choose to use and your tone of voice. You should listen to people's pitch, pace and choice of words and maintain relationships by matching them.

Practical things are important too, like the quality of the telephone line and using a headset so you are not restricted by the telephone or mobile. Make sure you're not going to be interrupted by visitors; get yourself a supply of drinks (remember to visit the bathroom before you start); have your phone on hands-free, so you can write notes. It could be helpful to first ask coachees about their own environment so you can get a picture of where they are; imagine yourself in that environment with them.

An advantage of telephone coaching would be that you could have reference material around you; this can be helpful, especially when you are just starting coaching. Another benefit can be a lessening of inhibitions if the coachee is not having to watch your body language too.

You should have an agenda and share it with the coachee. It is also worth considering recording the calls and possibly providing a transcript that can be sent as an audio file and a PDF transcription. There are tools that you can use such as Conference Genie, which is very effective (your organization may have facilities).

Whilst on the phone, you should focus and expect the other person to do the same. Concentrate purely on the conversation and don't be tempted to multi-task on the phone. Treat the telephone meeting just as you would treat a face-to-face meeting.

One proven approach that helps with coaching is the GROW model. GROW is an acronym standing for **G**oal – **R**eality – **O**ptions – **W**rap-up (and more recently I have seen the W stand for **W**ill). The model is a simple yet power-ful framework for structuring a coaching or mentoring session.

The GROW Model – for solving problems and achieving goals

The GROW model was developed in coaching during the late 1980s and has been extensively used ever since. The power of GROW is that it is easily understood, straightforward to apply and very thorough, and as a behav-ioural model it is suited to the world of work. In addition, once you have an understanding of how it works, it is possible to apply it to an amazing variety of issues in a very effective way. Even complex, multifaceted problems can be tackled with GROW and it often enables individuals to make progress on issues even when they have been stuck for a long time.

The GROW model works well because it provides a structured, effective process for goals and challenges. It enables you to break down an issue into its constituent parts. Once these are clear it becomes straightforward to develop solutions yourself, so it is likely you will be committed to carrying them through.

A useful metaphor for the GROW model (using Will as well as Wrap-up for the 'W') is when you plan an important overseas driving journey for a business meeting. First, you would start with a map and together with your colleague you would decide where they are going (their Goal) and establish where they currently are right now (their current Reality). Then you explore various ways (the Options) of making the journey from where they are to where they want to be. In the final step, establishing the Will, you ensure your team member is Willing and committed to making the journey and is prepared for the conditions and obstacles they may meet on their way; remember – 'where there is a will – there is a way!' Once they have finished planning the journey they will then need to Wrap-up, knowing that you have the journey well planned.

In its traditional application, the GROW model assumes that the coach is not an expert in the coachee's situation, and therefore the coach must act as an objective facilitator, helping the coachee select the best options and not offering advice or direction. However, when leaders coach their team members and they have relevant experience, expertise and often common sense, then I believe people would like to hear some practical suggestions and solutions that they can mull over and consider – or you can at least plant a seed in their mind. You then become more of a trainer or mentor.

It's your job to guide the selection of options that are best for your organization and the coachee and to ignore any options that may have negative consequences.

Having said that you must try and get the coachees to diagnose their own problem first and draw on their own resources to help themselves, as many people actually know the solution but it just needs teasing out of them. This way it becomes more of a collaboration between coach and coachees and the coachees will have more 'buy-in' to the solution if they are the ones who thought of it (or at least think they thought of it first). The approach also depends on the subject matter and whether it is something practical or personal.

You can use GROW for yourself or with the support of another person. However, working through a difficult issue with other people often helps, as they do not have the same emotional attachment that we have to our own issues.

Use the following steps to structure a GROW coaching session:

Establish the Goal

In order to have an effective coaching session you should have already established a rapport and built a relationship. Throughout the coaching session you should continue to mirror, match, pace and lead to maintain your rapport. Together with the coachee, you must define and agree a 'SMARTER' goal (detailed information on goal setting and how to write goals is also in *The Personal Assistant & Secretarial Handbook*, 2nd edition) or outcome to be achieved. In doing this, it is useful to ask questions like:

- How will you know that you have achieved that goal?
- How will you know the problem is solved?

Examine current Reality

Then you ask the coachee to describe their current Reality – where they are at now. This is a very important step: too often, people try to solve a problem without fully considering their starting point, and often they are missing some of the information they need to solve the problem effectively. As the coachee tells you about his or her current Reality, the solution may start to emerge. The use of open-ended questions is the primary tool that enables reality to be understood. The intention is to help the coachee to probe into things, see things clearly and specifically, clarifying meaning, strip away assumptions and judgements, use precise language and provide real-world examples.

Useful coaching questions include:

- What, who, when, how often?
- What is happening now?
- What is the effect or result of that?

Explore the Options

Once the coachee has explored the current Reality in rich detail, it's time to explore what is possible; your role is to help the coachee to generate and discuss as many options as possible to move forward and help solve the problem. This is a natural process of self-discovery and in most cases they will amaze you by their capability of seeing their way through issues. Let them talk as much as they want to and only add suggestions if appropriate. Start by asking open-ended questions, remembering that they may not be coming out with lots of new ideas but instead bringing forward previous thoughts into sharper focus; then you need to discuss which are desirable and which are not. After the baseline questions, coaches can become more creative with their questioning style. At this stage coachees would probably like to hear your perspective, especially if they can't think of any more solutions or the ones they have generated are inadequate. Your aim is to flush out a variety of options to be pinned down or discarded in the wrap-up phase.

Typical questions used to establish the options are:

- What are the benefits and downsides of each option?
- What if this or that constraint were removed?
- What factors will you use to weigh up the options?
- What else could you do?

Establish the Will and Wrap-up phase

By developing a goal, examining current reality and exploring the options, coachees will now have a good idea of how they can achieve their Goal. If they have several options that they are still considering then you can help them narrow these down by asking further questions. Ask them to describe the reason for their choice(s) of solution as it tests their thinking and provides greater clarity about the level of certainty and confidence they have in taking action. You can help them break down the action into specific steps and to seriously think about evaluating the implications of the action, its practicality, any obstacles that could arise and any support they may need. Now coachees need to commit to specific actions, writing their goals down and specifying when they will take each step, who will be involved and when they will be reviewed.

This is when taking a challenging approach can be supportive. Using a variety of closed questions and feedback can ensure that a coachee has thought of everything. In so doing, you will help them establish their will and motivation.

Useful questions:

- What could stop you moving forward?
- Will this address your goal?
- So what will you do now, and when?
- And how will you overcome it?
- How likely is this option to succeed?
- What else will you do?

A great way to practise using the model is to address your own challenges and issues. When you have a problem you can use the technique to coach yourself. By practising on your own challenges and issues, you will learn how to ask the most helpful and skilful questions. You will also be able to use the model in an unconscious-competence way (just as when you have been driving a car for years – you no longer have to think about how to do it).

The two most important skills for a coach are the ability to ask skilful questions and listen effectively, allowing the coachee to do most of the talking. I have added a comprehensive list of coaching questions for your use in Resource 4, 'Coaching questions'. You can download this from **www.suefrance.com** using the password at the beginning of the book. Remember that silence is valuable thinking time and you don't always have to fill silence with the next question.

Coaching however, is not just about asking questions and listening; it is also about summarizing what people have said, offering feedback, rephrasing, confirming, considering and sometimes getting them to reframe what they have said. Remember that coaching is always a conversation.

Using different frames

Representational systems are the way that we represent experience. They are typically described as visual, auditory and kinaesthetic (feelings). Reframing can be used in different ways, depending on our preferred representational system. When coaching it is easy to pick up the coachees' representational systems from the language they use. You can read more about this in *The Personal Assistant & Secretarial Handbook*, 2nd edition. Here are some examples.

- I **see** what you mean – **visual**.
- That **sounds** about right – **auditory**.
- I **feel** unsure about that – **kinaesthetic**.

Looking for patterns and repetition of visual, auditory and kinaesthetic words, as well as context and content, helps you to select the most helpful reframing tool for the coachee. Below are some examples and how they might be used.

A person who has a preference for a 'visual' representation will have created a picture in their mind's eye of a particular experience. As a coach you can suggest that they try to make the following changes to the image they have in their mind's eye and then reflect on how this alters their experience of the situation. If it is an experience they want to feel better about then ask them to:

'Change the picture'; if it's colour then change it to black and white; if it's bright then change it to being a dull picture; 'Making the picture smaller', 'Change the frame around the picture', 'Adjust the contrast', 'Add in some humorous imagery' etc.

If it is an image and experience that you want to remember, enhance and feel good about then you can:

'Change the Picture', 'Change the colour to vivid colours', 'Make it brighter', 'Making the picture larger', 'Change the frame around the picture', 'Adjust the contrast', 'Add in some humorous imagery' etc.

The new perspectives offered by these changes may influence the feelings that the coachee has about the situation. In this way a potentially daunting meeting with 'the boss', for example, can be adjusted so that it becomes a more pleasant experience or even one that the coachee looks forward to.

Reframing the internal dialogue

Our internal dialogue is the voice we hear in our heads; it can be positive or negative so when coaching you can ask coachees to think about what they are saying to themselves at certain points during the coaching session. This helps them to notice what their inner voice is saying and whether it is helping or hindering their progress. For coaches with 'auditory' preferences, you can ask them to change the negative thoughts to positive ones; ask them to try the following and reflect on how this alters their perception:

> *'Turn the volume up or down'; 'Add some funny music'; 'Change the pace or tone of the voice.'*

As with changing the picture and the sound, this process also has an impact on the feelings about the experience.

Looking at the situation from a different perspective

We get bound up with the events, issues and concerns about how to tackle a relationship or a situation in our lives. This often leaves us trapped in a cycle of non-productive behaviour. A useful way of helping coachees to reframe these types of situation is to get them to view their experience or event from another person's shoes, often described as being in second position or even third position. You should ask questions like: 'If you were the other person, what would you notice about your behaviour/approach/manner?' 'If you were an observer watching the event/discussion, what would you notice?' 'What would your mentor/manager/best friend/coach do in this situation?' It is also useful to ask coachees to physically sit in different seats as they do this exercise, imagining that they are someone else and truly empathizing and observing what is going on from somebody else's point of view.

The process of stepping into another's shoes can help to take the heat out of a potentially fraught situation, help the coachee to see a relationship in a different way, identify alternative ways of tackling a problem and offer a variety of different ways of responding to situations.

Wheel of life/timeline

The 'Wheel of life' is an extremely powerful coaching tool for helping people see where they are at currently and where they want to be – see Figure 6.1 (which you can also download from **www.suefrance.com**, called Resource 8). This particular 'Wheel of life' concentrates on your work–life balance so that you can take some time out to think about yourself. It will also help you clarify priorities for goal setting. You can use Resource 5

FIGURE 6.1   Wheel of life

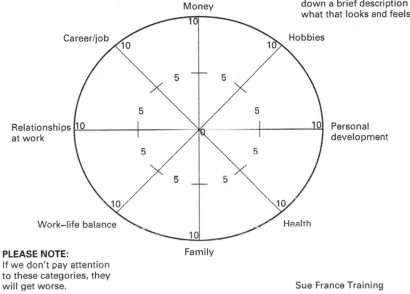

Mark each area on a scale of 1–10 where you believe you are right now in terms of satisfaction.

Wheel of Life

Categories for improvement

For each category imagine how it would be at a 10, if you were feeling total satisfaction and achievement. Write down a brief description of what that looks and feels like.

PLEASE NOTE:
If we don't pay attention to these categories, they will get worse.

Sue France Training

in conjunction with Resource 8 to write down a brief description for each category as if you were feeling total satisfaction and achievement. Imagine what it would look and feel like and what you would hear if each category was marked with a 10! This downloadable resource can easily be changed to suit any adaptation of the wheel that you choose. See Resource 6, 'Blank Wheel of Life – to use creatively'.

Instructions on how to use the Wheel of life tool

Think about what success feels like in the different areas (career/job, money, relationships at work, hobbies, personal development, family, work–life balance and health), then rank your level of satisfaction with each area of your life by placing a value between 1 (dissatisfied) and 10 (extremely satisfied) against each area to show how satisfied you are currently with these elements of your life. This will be portrayed by drawing a line across each segment.

An example of how the wheel may look once charted can be found in Resource 6, 'Blank Wheel of life'.

Studying the Wheel of life that you have charted, you will see where you may need to spend some time working on it to improve the situation.

Ask yourself the following questions:

- Are there any surprises for you?
- How do you feel about your life as you look at your Wheel?
- How do you currently spend time in these areas?
- How would you like to spend time in these areas?
- Which of these elements would you most like to improve?
- How could you make space for these changes?
- Can you prioritize which you will work on in order?
- Can you effect the necessary changes on your own?
- What help and cooperation from others might you need?
- What would a score of 10 look like?
- What would you need to do to make each area a score of 10?

Adapting the Wheel of life to suit your needs

The Wheel of life can be adapted and used in many different ways in coaching others and yourself. For this purpose you can use Resource 6, which is a blank Wheel of life that can be completed to suit your requirements, taking into consideration some of the ideas below or any ideas you can think of that suit the person you are coaching and/or for yourself.

When coaching others you may wish to collaborate with the coachee and decide on what each section should be called (ie the areas you wish to work on). Alternatively you may wish to pre-fill some of the sections and leave some blank sections for coachees to complete thereby getting their buy-in.

The Wheel of life as a performance management tool

You could use the Wheel of life as a performance management tool and complete the sections to show how you perceive the person you are coaching/ mentoring.

Alternatively you can use it in a 360° appraisal and have the boss as well as peers and anyone reporting to them/you complete a Wheel of life for them/you. The people you ask to complete this should be trustworthy and those whose opinions they/you value; they should know the coachee/mentee (or you) well as it can be helpful to see how others perceive you. The coachee/mentee (or you) can complete the Wheel of life and compare it with the ones others complete on them/you. This will give an all rounded overall view of how others perceive how you are performing and how they/you perceive they/you are performing, which can be quite enlightening – which is why you have to trust and value the opinion of the people completing this for you. The coachee/mentee should be allowed to choose the people who complete this for them.

The sections for a performance management tool will be the skills and competencies used in your role and can be as detailed as you like, or have other Wheel of life exercises with 'chunked down' (detailed) sections.

For example: You could have a 'Competency skills Wheel of life' with the following eight sections: Leadership skills, Communication skills, Social media skills, Stress management skills, Networking skills, Organizational skills, Public relationship skills and Technology skills etc.

Each area could be broken down, and using a blank wheel you could input the following sections for a 'Leadership skills Wheel of life': Leadership could be 'chunked down' for example to: Problem solving, Decision making, Delegating, Negotiating, Emotional intelligence, Persuasive and influencing skills, Coaching and mentoring skills and Motivational skills etc.

A 'Communication skills Wheel of life' could be 'chunked down' to the following skills: Questioning skills, Listening skills, Body language skills, Business writing skills, Assertiveness, Giving and receiving feedback skills, Linguistic skills (eg NLP and visual, auditory and kinaesthetic) and Presentation skills.

Again each of these areas could be further 'chunked down' in, for example, a 'Presentation Skills Wheel of Life': Understanding learning styles, Research and preparation skills, Continual self-development, Understanding personality styles, Handling difficult people skills, Motivational skills, Confidence skills and Time management skills.

> Remember: 'If you always do what you've always done, then you'll always get what you always got' and the only way to make a difference is to TAKE ACTION.

Yes you've guessed it – you can also use the Wheel of life to help you take action!

How to communicate with different personality and behavioural styles

This chapter will enable you to be an effective team member, supervisor and leader. It will show you how to learn about and understand yourself as well as teach you how you to:

- interact with others;
- communicate effectively;
- motivate people;
- get the best out of different types of personalities and behavioural styles.

Have you ever tried to communicate something to someone and they just don't understand what you mean?

Or perhaps you cannot understand why someone should act in a certain way or say the things they do? Some people simply understand immediately, whilst for others there can be continuous misunderstandings. Of course there are several things that can affect this, including how busy you or they are.

Filters and perception

We use our past experiences as the filter through how we judge other people's behaviours. Our primitive reaction is to decide quickly whether someone is a friend or foe so we stereotype people, judging them by how they stand, how they dress, their hairstyle and so on. Our perception profoundly changes how we feel about people.

We need to understand why we understand and perceive others the way we do and find out why other people do and say what they do and say. We can do this by fully exploring the alternatives of what we see, hear and feel and what maybe we could see, hear and feel if we looked at it differently. The ability to see things from the point of view of another is a key skill in understanding people.

One way to accomplish this is to use the NLP technique of the 'Three Perceptual Positions' as follows.

Three-perceptual-positioning technique

This technique is very useful when there is a conflict as it allows us to have a multiple perspective in any situation so that we can have greater understanding, empathy and flexibility. You don't need the person you have a conflict with to be present as it is an exercise where you can figure out a solution by yourself.

Place three chairs in a circle – each chair is a 'perceptual position' and you have to sit in each chair/perceptual position for each stage as follows:

First position (sit in first chair)

Looking at the world from your own point of view, through your own eyes. This is your own perceptual position as you really experience it: feel it, see it, and hear it. You should be fully in it and living it as if it is happening right now. You should be totally associated and not taking account of anyone else's point of view.

Think: How does this affect me?
Shake yourself and disassociate yourself from the first position.

Second position (sit in second chair)

This is the perceptual position of another person. Looking through another person's eyes, appreciating the other point of view. How would this appear to them? This position can be in direct communication with first position. That is, if you adopted second position, and spoke to yourself in first position, you would address yourself as 'you'.

The stronger the rapport you have with another person, the easier it will be for you to appreciate their reality of the world and how they perceive things – remember we all delete, distort and generalize the same scenario completely differently from each other. You really have to 'get into their skin' and think how are they seeing this problem? What do they feel? What do they hear?

Shake yourself and disassociate yourself from the second position.

Third position (sit in third chair)

This is about observing the feedback of first and second positions from a dissociated position. You see the world from an outside point of view, as an independent observer with no personal involvement in the situation. How would this look to someone who is not involved? This is a useful position for gathering information and noticing relationship dynamics going on between them. In third position, if you were to refer to yourself in the first or the second position, you'd use third person pronouns such as 'he', 'she' or 'they'.

This creates an objective viewpoint from which you can generate and evaluate some useful choices in a difficult situation.

All three positions are equally important and the purpose is to be able to move between them freely, taking the information gained from each, to see if you have gleaned any new insights from the different positions; if you need to go and sit back in one of the seats again then do. You must only state from that other person's point of view, or from the observer when sitting in the appropriate chair/position.

Your basic personality will also have an effect on the way you think, perceive things and communicate. There are several models and systems that help to explain our behaviours, the words we choose to use and our preferred style of communicating.

I have chosen the following three models of behaviour, personality styles, ways of thinking and communicating that are extremely useful in helping me to understand myself and others. They are also quite fun to use:

- TetraMap® – Behavioural model – Four elements – Earth, Air, Water and Fire;

- Disc® model;
- Transactional Analysis – The ego states.

Behavioural model

Background

In the 1920s, Carl Jung, a Swiss psychologist, conducted in-depth work into psychological types that became the foundation for many works to follow, for example Myers-Briggs, Keirsey, Lowry, Berens and TetraMap®. Jung described the four personality types as being Intellect directed, Body directed, Feeling directed and Intuition directed.

Extravert vs introvert

Carl Jung's most important contribution to the study of human personality was his theory of introversion. In common terms, introversion relates to reserved personalities and extraversion to outgoing personalities. However the types can also be described as how individuals who are energized (ie extraverts) tend to seek stimulation from outside themselves while introverts seek stimulation from within.

Introverts tend to be more focused on what they are doing or thinking. They look at a subject in more depth. They can be quieter, but not necessarily all the time. They are more likely to have only a few people that they call their close friends.

Extraverts get their energy from the outside world and other people. Having to sit quietly by themselves is what drains their energy. They need to socialize with people and they have many close friends and acquaintances. When reading the descriptions of the temperaments later on in the chapter, remember that being introverted or extraverted will modify the way people express their temperaments.

As suggested by Linda Berens in the late 1990s, given our 'true self' and our 'developed self', we are able to behave and react in a variety of ways in different situations or contexts. She states that we have the choice of giving in to our true self or following our developed self or selecting an appropriate contextual response. I believe that developing successful relationships is about choosing the way we respond.

In each of the three following behavioural tools, not everyone will fit the descriptions all of the time. In fact we all have every element or behavioural style within us that we can and do use. However, one element or behaviour style tends to be dominant – a set of behaviours that we are more adept at, feel comfortable with and use frequently.

After reading this chapter you will have a better insight and understanding of yourselves as well as of those around you, and in particular your boss. Having this knowledge will allow you to 'read' their verbal and non-verbal clues to their personalities and behavioural styles so you can adapt your behaviours in order to influence, persuade and be better able to communicate on the same wavelength, and therefore reduce conflict and build excellent working relationships.

TetraMap® – Behavioural model

TetraMap® is a registered trademark of TetraMap® International in New Zealand, UK and other countries. The following content is the author's interpretation of TetraMap® and is reproduced with permission from TetraMap® International.

TetraMap® was designed by Yoshimi and Jon Brett in New Zealand in 2000 and was originally designed to reduce conflict in the workplace. It can also be used as a tool for improving behaviour and performance, planning and project management, finding team solutions, setting short and medium-term visions and helping leaders to lead.

TetraMap® helps to shift mindsets in a quick and simple way, resulting in improved communication and relationships. It helps people to work together better whilst accelerating positive change.

How TetraMap® can help executive assistants and office managers be leaders in their everyday role

Using the power of metaphor, TetraMap® explores four diverse perspectives of people's behaviours by mapping the four elements of Earth, Air, Water and Fire onto a tetrahedron shape (four-sided pyramid). This shape demonstrates interdependence and structural integrity, just as we work interdependently of each other and, hopefully, with integrity. What makes it different from other behavioural models is that there are no opposites.

Understanding the elements, coupled with your skill to respond rather than react, is the epitome of flexibility and can save you from becoming stressed. Meet Earth with Earth firmness and focus, meet Air with Air logic and questions, meet Water with caring and feelings, and meet Fire with hope and possibilities.

We should not describe people as Earth, Air, Water or Fire people as we are much more complex than our dominant behavioural styles, but we can talk about Earth, Air, Water and Fire elements.

To enable you to understand the different behavioural styles of the four elements I am going to set out two different case studies and describe the possible reactions of each element. By reading through the following element descriptions and their reactions, you may recognize yourself and may be able to identify your boss(es), members of your own team and colleagues. Remember that normally you will have one or two preferred elemental styles although we all have all four elements within us.

- **Earth elements** are predominantly left-brainers and task focused. They are good with numbers, language and logic and at organizing others, although they can be perceived as blunt. They may also be aggressive and appear to bulldoze their way through problems.

- **Air elements** are also left-brainers and are therefore task focused and good with numbers, languages and logic, and at organizing others. They are also known for being creative.

- **Water elements** are important in holding teams together so that they work efficiently and effectively without conflict. They are patient, reflective and resourceful and make good listeners. Water elements are right-brain focused and people orientated.

- **Fire elements** appreciate possibilities and tend to be spontaneous. They are optimistic and tend to look on the positive side of life and inspire others to see bright futures and think about the 'big picture'. Fire elements are often colourful, love variety, and are sociable and always ready for a party. They are right-brain focused and people orientated.

CASE STUDY 1

It has been announced that a charity event has to be organized, and that is all the information that has been given. The following is how the different elements may react to the news that they are to organize a charity event, and how their preferred style can contribute to the success of the event.

The earth elements

- Would have made the decision to host the event in the first place.

- Will already be thinking about potential business or networking opportunities that may come out of it.

- Will provide a brief that is short and without detail; however, if you ask questions they will provide structure and detail to provide good results.

- Are goal orientated – they would measure the success of the charity event by the amount of money raised.

The air elements

- Are internally focused and will sit down to plan the event, making detailed lists and schedules.

- Will anticipate any hiccups and have multiple back-up plans in place.

- Are not prone to being emotional so others may perceive them negatively, as they worry more about resources than who will benefit from the charity.

- Appreciate clarity and will ask lots of questions relating to cost, practicality, insurance etc.

- Will be on board with the project and give it 100 per cent as that is what they have been asked to do.

- Are creative, and will come up with good ideas on how to raise money.

The water elements

- Would love the concept of organizing a charity event as it involves helping people.

- Will want time to consult everyone about which charity to support.

- Take a long time to make a decision, as they take everyone's thoughts, suggestions and concerns on board.

- Are calm. They will pull out all the stops to make sure the event goes to plan without stress.

- Would aim for a smooth running event, want everyone to have a wonderful time and want to make lots of money to help the charity.

The fire elements

- Would be very enthusiastic and already thinking about the venue, balloons, beautiful invitations, what outfit they will wear and about standing on stage to greet all the guests, as they love to be the centre of attention.

- Will want to get everyone involved and excited about the event.

- Do not like boundaries so would have to be carefully managed by others to make sure they stay on budget.

- Will use their hands a lot when talking about their ideas and are easily distracted.

- Will enjoy the whole idea of organizing a charity event and will even organize a celebration event when it's successful.

CASE STUDY 2

If your boss, team members or colleagues had a preference for one of the four elements of TetraMap® you will need to understand and learn how best to communicate with them. The advice below will help you to influence and persuade them:

How to influence preferred Earth Elemental style

When you talk to an Earth Element, they want to know what's in it for them and what the purpose is. You should be firm, assertive, direct and to the point, and at the same time be confident both in what you say and how you say it. Your body language should be congruent to what you are saying and your head should be held high. You should make eye contact when you speak directly with them. If you are going into a meeting with an Earth Element, make sure you have just a page of bullet points prepared and keep it short and to the point. They don't want long reports but prefer tables illustrating what you mean or pie charts that are quick and easy to read. They simply want to get the job done! They want you to think ahead for them and be ready for any eventuality. Admire their achievements, their leadership and their status if appropriate.

Avoid long-winded conversations with an Earth Element as they are not interested in small talk about how their weekend went. Neither are they interested in asking you about yours! They do not want you to ramble on about things or be touchy-feely. Don't take it personally that they are not interested or that they may be blunt – it is just their style so don't take it to heart. They can lack empathy and self-awareness and you need to be aware of this, especially if your preference is the Water Element, who are the most people oriented.

Your Earth Element boss is motivated by a measurable success and would want you to align your goals with theirs and the organization's. They want you to help them achieve their goals, especially as they may lack persistence.

Questions you might ask an Earth Element in order to 'connect' with them and guide the conversation to a positive outcome:

- What specifically are the results you are aiming for?

- This is a big challenge – how can we face this head on together?

- This may be a bit more risky but what do you think about...?

How to influence preferred Air Elemental style

As time frames are important to Air Elements, discuss what needs to be prioritized in order to reach their objectives and deadlines. Make sure you clearly communicate lots of detail to them in a logical sequence and speak slowly and precisely so they clearly understand. Air Elements could be inclined to micromanage unless you give them constant feedback and the detail they crave. Let them know you understand how the details fit into the big picture. When you are listening to an Air Element, stay focused on what they are saying, take notes and ask questions for clarity. They want your help to achieve accurate results. They like tidiness and precision, so if your desk is messy they may think you are out of control. Recognize and acknowledge the need for structure and rules.

They do not want you to demand immediate action but prefer to have time to think things through from every angle – including the human angle. They don't want you to exaggerate or overgeneralize. You will lose them if you change subjects too quickly.

Clarify the desired result and outcomes, and support Air Elements by making positive suggestions. Encourage them and their abilities by letting them know you know they can do it.

Questions you might ask an Air Element in order to 'connect' with them and guide the conversation to a positive outcome:

- What do you think about this?

- How much more time would you need to...?

- Can you explain the logic behind this?

How to influence preferred Water Elemental style

Water Elements would like you to communicate calmly and considerately and be aware of their feelings. Speak slowly and softly, smile with your eyes and look as if you care. They are kind and sensitive and expect kindness in return. Explain what you need and why, and help them to make decisions. Admire their hard work, loyalty and kindness, and remember to thank them for their efforts. You should value their contributions and include them in everything. Keep it personal and explain values and meanings when you give advice. They are 'people-people' and always think of others. Be open and interested, listen attentively and build trust, which helps to build strong working relationships. Be reassuring and supportive, steer away from conflict and consider what might be fair and equitable. Ask them about their family and tell them about yours as they are genuinely interested. Water Elements love to chat and may get carried away, so you may have to steer them back on track.

Water Elements do not want you to be too loud, bold, demanding or discourteous. Give them as much of your time as you can as they love to be around people, and also give them time for processing their thoughts. Be prepared to share your thoughts and ideas with them.

Questions you might ask a Water Element in order to 'connect' with them and guide the conversation to a positive outcome:

- How do you feel about...?

- What are the steps you would take to overcome this?

- Shall we send a survey out to get everyone's buy-in first?

How to influence preferred Fire Elemental style

Enthusiastically communicate with Fire Elements and speak quickly, varying your intonation. Smile and inspire them, point them towards a bright future and give them hope. Keep your energy up, give options and remain positive. Have fun with Fire Elements and enjoy the celebrations. Give them the big picture and not too much detail. Try not to set them boundaries or structure them. Be animated when you talk to them and be optimistic and even adventurous. They want you to be open to ideas and to be trusting. They love feedback and the more positive the better, though constructive criticism is much appreciated. Inject a sense of fun where appropriate to keep things alive and moving. Have new ideas and be inspirational and visual. Focus on possibilities and opportunities. Admire their ideas, creativity and their popularity. They want you to recognize their efforts and they would love it if you praised them publicly as that would motivate them. When you communicate, with them, they need positivity and excitement to keep their interest.

When you are creating presentations for them, make them as interesting and 'whizzy' as possible. They want you to be open to new ideas and make suggestions where appropriate.

Questions you might ask a Fire Element in order to 'connect' with them and guide the conversation to a positive outcome:

- What possibilities and opportunities can you see in this?

- How will this help us to reach our vision?

- Shall we celebrate the end of this project?

The TetraMap® process consists of completing a short profiling questionnaire, which I cannot reproduce here for copyright reasons but Certified TetraMap® facilitators (like myself) can take you through the process. See www.tetramap.com for more information.

TetraMap® enables individuals to 'see' themselves as others see them and to develop strategies for reducing any negative impact on teams of their strengths and enthusiasm, while increasing and enhancing the positive impact of their unique contributions.

DiSC® Model

Dr William Moulton Marston was the American Psychologist whose work inspired the development of the modern 'DiSC® model' and associated solutions and tools. Marston explored our different perceptions of the environment around us and our responses to it. He observed that some people perceive themselves as having more power and control over their environment than others. He also noticed that some people perceive the environment to be more favourable and 'friendly' than others.

These observations led him to define four basic styles of thinking, feeling and behaving – DiSC® – 'D' which stands for 'Dominance', 'I' for Influence,

'S' for 'Steadiness' and 'C' for 'Conscientious'. Each style has 'highs' and 'lows', resulting in eight main behavioural styles.

> Julie French, a Certified Trainer in 'Everything DiSC' says 'Understanding and using DiSC® brings a new level of awareness that helps us recognize, appreciate (even laugh about!) our differences. When we know "what planet" the other person is on, we can smile about what we are noticing, acknowledge the differences and even enjoy the whole experience!'

To illustrate the model I want you to think about a specific situation and a specific person you have been in conflict with:

- How were they communicating with you?
- How were they approaching the issue, task or problem in hand?

Dominance ('D')

If they were leaning towards the 'D' or Dominance style, you might have noticed that their main priorities are getting results, taking action and challenge.

They might have come across as loud, competitive, fast-paced, interrupting, direct, independent, questioning, assertive, blunt, forceful, wanting to take charge, results-oriented. You may have perceived that they have no regard for your feelings, and could be insensitive and lack patience.

If you want to communicate effectively with the Dominance style then you should be brief and to the point, and respect the fact that they need to feel in control and that you understand that failure is not an option. Show them you are competent and focus on the results and the fact that they can be measured. Accept their bluntness and don't expect empathy as it's just their style.

Influence ('I')

If they were leaning more towards the 'I' or Influence style, you might have noticed that their main priorities are taking action, enthusiasm and collaboration.

They might have come across as optimistic, lively, persuasive, emotional, seeking recognition, fun oriented, easily distracted, talkative, informal, seeking variety, unfocused, full of new ideas. They can also be impulsive and disorganized. If you know them well you may also have noticed that they fear loss of control, being taken advantage of and vulnerability.

If you want to communicate effectively with the Influencing style, then you should show enthusiasm and acknowledge their feelings and have a sense of fun about you. At the same time you should reassure them that they are not being taken advantage of and that they are still in control.

Steadiness ('S')

If they were leaning more towards the 'S' or Steadiness style, you might have noticed that their main priorities are collaboration, support and stability.

They might have come across as quiet, kind, dependable, methodical, going with the flow, good listeners, following rather than leading, indecisive, team focused, patient and accommodating. They can seem insecure, often related to change or uncertainty. If you know them well you may have noticed that they have a fear of a loss of harmony and normally like to keep the peace.

If you want to communicate effectively with them then you should focus on the needs of the team, avoid unnecessary changes and conflict, share information, let them know what's coming and avoid pushing or rushing. Praise them for their positive ideas and help them to implement them.

Conscientious ('C')

If they were leaning more towards the 'C' or Conscientious style, you might have noticed that their main priorities are stability, accuracy and challenge.

They might have come across as cautious, pedantic, systematic, reserved, formal, paying attention to detail, private, preferring to work on their own, having high standards, precise, negative, focused on facts, logical, evidence based. They dislike conflict so will try tactics to avoid it. Sometimes they can be perceived as negative or cold.

If you want to communicate effectively with them then you should avoid displays of emotion, be precise and focused and have facts and reasons to hand, show you value high standards, demonstrate your dependability and be prepared. They like to have clear parameters laid out and standard operating procedures. You should also allow them time to think, ask questions and check before they make decisions.

By understanding the DiSC® model you will have an insight and awareness to 'decode' these uncomfortable situations and to fully appreciate the clash of needs that is often happening.

Think about what your style is and think about how each of the groups may perceive you; from there you can work out the best way to communicate.

For clarity TetraMap® can be mapped against DiSC® as follows: Dominance (D) is similar to Earth, Influence (I) is similar to Fire, Steadiness (S) is similar to Water and Conscientious (C) is similar to Air.

Transactional Analysis – the ego-state (or Parent–Adult–Child) model

In addition to the analysis of the interactions between individuals, Transactional Analysis (TA) also involves the identification of the 'ego states' that lie behind each and every transaction.

Have you ever thought that you were communicating in one way and later learned that you were perceived in a completely different way? Have you ever asked a question at a meeting and then felt about five years old? Have you ever told someone off and then felt like kicking yourself for it later? Do you often find yourself feeling defensive about your ideas or point of view? Do you feel that you have to take care of too many people who should be taking care of themselves? Have you ever used the same technique to get what you want from your boss that you used as a child with your parents? Now you will understand why you do and say what you do and say.

Transactional Analysis (or TA as it is often called) is a model of people and relationships that was developed by Dr Eric Berne. It is based on two notions: first that we have three parts or 'ego-states' to our 'personality' (parent, adult and child), and second that we communicate (transact) as a parent would communicate, as a child would communicate or as an adult communicates.

As a practising psychiatrist in Carmel, California, Berne treated hundreds of patients. He consistently noted that all people change over the course of a conversation. The changes would not necessarily be just verbal; they could involve facial expressions, body language, body temperature and many other non-verbal cues.

The following are detailed descriptions of the three ego states, and you may recognize your own behaviours as well as the behaviour of others that are portrayed some of the time.

Parent

The Parent represents a massive collection of memories of external events experienced or perceived as a child.

When in Parent mode we talk to people as if they are children. This behaviour comes from what we observed as children in our parents and other figures of authority. The Parent state is where people behave, feel and think in response to an unconscious mimicking of how their parents (or other parental figures) acted, or how they interpreted their parent's actions. For example, a person may shout at someone out of frustration because they learned from an influential figure in childhood the lesson that this seemed to be a way of relating that worked.

It is worth noting that, while remembering these events, the young child has no way to filter the data; the events are 'recorded' in his or her brain without question and without analysis. You can consider that these events are imposed on a child. The Controlling Parent says things like 'Never talk to strangers'; 'Don't show off'; 'Always eat with your mouth closed'; 'Look both ways before you cross the street' and 'Sit up straight'.

There are two forms of Parent state that we can use:

- The **Nurturing Parent** is a loving parent, permission-giving, encouraging, security-giving, caring and concerned. They seek to keep you contented and encourage you, offering a safe haven to calm people's troubles. They can appear comforting, making excuses and making allowances for you, and can even be suffocating. They gesture with open arms and are likely to give you a pat on the shoulder or back for doing a good job. They may call you 'poppet' or 'sweetheart' and say things like 'are you ok?'; 'I'll take care of it for you'; 'don't worry about it'; 'well done'; 'what a shame'; 'take care'; 'remember to...'; 'I'll help you...' and 'It won't take me long to...' They simply want to look after you and make sure everything is alright for you. They use words like 'good' and 'nice' and will often smile.

- The **Controlling Parent** is a restricting parent who disciplines you and tries to make you do what they want you to do, perhaps transferring values or beliefs. They may wag their finger and their eyebrows may go up or they may have their hands on their hips when they talk when in this state. They may also pound the table or shake their heads. Their facial expressions may be scowling, hostile, disapproving and frowning. They lay down the law and can lecture you. They can appear patronizing, sneering, condescending, judgemental, concerned, strict, sometimes sarcastic and even disgusted. They will say things like 'You must always...'; 'make sure you...'; 'you should...'; 'how could you be so stupid as to...'; 'it's dangerous to...'; 'we have got certain standards and procedures to follow.' They use words like 'right/wrong', 'good/bad' and 'never/always'.

When we feel, think, talk and behave in the way we remember our parents doing, then we are adopting the Parent state. So at work we might say things like 'The way to act in this situation is...' (Controlling Parent) or 'Leave it to me I'll fix it' (Nurturing Parent).

When you are in a Controlling Parent state, you will have a strong personality and probably will find it fairly easy to get people to do what you want. In this state you have to be careful to not make enemies and you should try and give people the impression that you do respect them.

When you are in a Nurturing Parent state you can create a strong positive impression being seen as a helpful and caring person. However an exaggerated concern for others can inhibit them and even take away their influence. It can also result in you taking on too much yourself impinging on your time in a desire to do too much for others.

When you express your ego state you:

Give advice	Nurture and protect
Discipline	Make rules and regulations
Criticize	Teach
Moralize	Judge

Adult

In the Adult state we behave much more logically, basing what we do and say on facts and an objective analysis of the situation. It is the 'grown up', rational, thoughtful calm person – we talk reasonably and neither try to control nor react aggressively towards others. The Adult is comfortable with him/her and is or should be our 'ideal self'. We can think through different situations, be able to assert ourselves and negotiate effectively, leading to clearly effective workable solutions.

The Adult stance is normally standing up straight with good eye contact and head held high. The facial expression would be thoughtful and alert.

Understanding Transactional Analysis will help you to learn to strengthen the Adult state within you, which is the ideal state. It is often the attitude rather than the actual words that reveal the different states.

Adults are likely to use what, why, when, where, who, how questioning and find out whether the matter in hand is practical and logical. Their attitude is one of being interested, detached and evaluative. It is the mature and intentional part of the personality where our actions and words are sensible and well considered, as opposed to the almost automatic reactions of the Parent or Child states. In the Adult state we collate information, evaluate it, work out possible solutions and resolve problems in a logical and calm way. We concentrate on the facts rather than emotional feelings and prejudices.

Adopting the Adult stage as your dominant behaviour can be advantageous in many circumstances. In difficult, stressful or conflict situations you should stick to the facts, be sensible and analytical, looking at things from everyone's perception and viewpoint in order to make a rational decision. If you are respected as a well-balanced person who can think logically and objectively then people will turn to you for advice. However, if you are in the Adult state too much, there is a risk that you will not have much fun.

You use your Adult state when you:

Plan	Evaluate
Check alternatives	Estimate probabilities
Make decisions	Set limits
Reason.	

Child

Stored in the Child state are the emotions or feelings 'recorded' in our brains from our own childhood and upbringing, and we behave, feel and think similarly to the way we did in childhood. For example, a person who receives a poor evaluation at work may respond by looking at the floor and crying or pouting, as they used to when scolded as a child. Conversely, a person who receives a good evaluation may respond with a broad smile and a joyful gesture of thanks. The Child is the source of emotions, creation, recreation, spontaneity and intimacy.

There are three types of Child state that we use: our patterns of behaviour, feelings and ways of thinking, which can be functional (beneficial or positive) or dysfunctional (counterproductive or negative). Sometimes it is stated that there are only two types of child state: the Free Child and the Adaptive Child, but here I have separated the Free Child state into two parts:

- The **Natural Child (Free Child)** is largely not self-aware; in this state we are carefree, playful, uninhibited (and undisciplined) and creative. The Natural child is energetic, loose limbed and casual, and speaks with a loud tone. When we are in a Free Child state, we have a joyful twinkling expression on our faces.

- The **Little Professor** (also part of the Free Child state) is the curious and exploring Child who tries out new things (often much to their Controlling Parent's annoyance). When we are in our Little Professor state, we are intuitive and understand things and people in a way that is different from Adult logic.

- The **Adaptive Child** reacts to the world around them. When we are in this state, we either change ourselves to fit in or rebel. We can be obedient, resentful or manipulative. In this state we may become withdrawn, going quiet after being told off, or we may become angry. An example would be someone stomping out of a meeting and slamming the door behind them! You would say things like 'please let me...'; 'I won't!'; 'It's not fair' 'You always try to...', 'I can't...', and 'why me again?', 'please' and 'thank you'. Someone in an adaptive child state might say they are not going to listen to you, agree with you or do what you want. They can rebel indirectly by forgetting, procrastinating and doing things differently or badly. The gestures of the adaptive child could be slumped, dejected, nail-biting or eyelash-fluttering. They could use tone of voice in a whining, sulky, defiant or in an aggressive way. Their facial expressions could be fearful, pouting, wide-eyed or innocent.

If you spend time in the Child state as your dominant state then you will have intuition, spontaneity and inspiration, which are all useful traits when you want to be creative and generate ideas. You will be able to inspire and motivate people emotionally to get them to accept your proposals and suggestions. However be careful not to be perceived as being aggressive, resentful and sometimes selfish.

The Child state is observable when you show:

Fear	Compliance
Curiosity	Aggression
Creativity	Sulking
Trust	Self-indulgence
Anger	Rebelliousness

In an attempt to explain Transactional Analysis, Dr Thomas Harris developed the following simplified summary.

Parent   –   taught concept

Adult   –   learned concept

Child   –   felt concept

We each have internal models of parents, children and also adults, and we play these roles with one another in our relationships. We even do it with ourselves, in our internal conversations. They all have their uses, have their strengths and weaknesses and are appropriate in different circumstances. For example Free Child (Natural and Little Professor) is particularly useful if we want to generate lots of new ideas in a brainstorming (brain-dumping) session. Using the concept of ego states gives us a method of checking our behaviour and consciously selecting the most appropriate option for our current goal.

Analysing transactions (communication between people)

When analysing transactions it is important to note that when identifying which ego states are involved we have to take into consideration not only what is said but how it is being said: for example, accents on certain words, tone and volume of voice, the choice of words used, non-verbal body language such as facial expressions and so on.

Types of transactions

The first thing you say is called the 'stimulus'. If someone says to you 'You look good today' (you perceive it as an Adult comment) – and what you say back is the 'response' – 'Thank you' (Adult).

You have to recognize there are different types of dynamics – it's about perception. If someone answers you back in the Child state, think about why they answered in that way. It's because of their perception of you. If you have just said something they perceive as Controlling Parent (ie judgemental or criticizing), they hear the Controlling Parent in you and can come back with a Child response.

Their filters and their past can cause them to misunderstand and mistranslate your words, and thereby cross-miscommunication begins and conflict can occur.

For example: someone might say to you 'You look good today' (and you perceive it as Controlling Parent) and you reply 'Oh, this old thing – I have had it ages and I just threw it on' (Child).

There are basically three kinds of transactions:

- reciprocal/complementary (the simplest);
- crossed transactions;
- ulterior.

Reciprocal/complementary transactions

These transactions occur when both people are at the same level (Parent talking to Parent, etc.). For example:

A: Have you been able to write the report yet? (Adult to Adult)
B: Yes – I'm about to e-mail it to you. (Adult to Adult)

A: What do you think of the new filing system I've devised? (Adult to Adult)
B: Tell me more about how it works – is it colour coded? (Adult to Adult)

A: Would you like to skip this meeting and go watch a film with me instead? (Child to Child)
B: I'd love to – I don't want to work anymore, what should we go and see? (Child to Child)

Crossed transactions and conflict

Conflict arises and problems occur in crossed transactions, where each is talking to a different ego state. For example, an adult supervisor/leader may take on the Parent role, and tell an adult employee off as if s/he was a Child.
For example:

A: Have you been able to write that report yet? (Adult to Adult)
B: Will you stop hassling me? I'll do it in my own time! (Adaptive Child to Parent)

A: What do you think of the new filing system I've devised? (Adult to Adult)
B: It must have taken you ages to do all that – how clever of you. (Nurturing Parent to Child)

A: What do you think of the new filing system I've devised? (Adult to Adult)
B: If I were you I would spend less time messing about on things that don't have top priority. (Controlling Parent to Child)

Crossed transactions are likely to produce problems in the workplace. Sometimes a message is sent from one ego state and the sender expects it to be sent back from the same ego state, but it's sent back from a different one. The transaction is crossed; communication is non-effective.

A: You messed that document up – it's full of errors and typos. (Controlling Parent – Child)

They will have expected a response like 'I am sorry, I'll make sure it won't happen again'. Instead they get the response:

B: That's rubbish, it's your fault because you can't understand or use correct English. (Controlling Parent to Child)

A: The deadline is tomorrow and we will need to stay an extra half an hour to finish it. (Adult – Adult)

Expecting them to say 'Yes that's fine I know it has to be done'. Instead they get the response:

B: If you didn't always leave things to the last minute that could have been avoided! (Controlling Parent to Child)

The Parent is either nurturing or controlling and often speaks to the Child, who is either Adaptive or 'Natural/Free' in their response. When both people talk as a Parent to the other's Child, their wires get crossed and conflict results.

The Nurturing Parent in a warm friendly tone naturally talks to the Natural/Free Child within you and may ask for some solutions, ideas and creativity that the Natural/Free Child will respond to. The Controlling Parent naturally talks to the Adaptive Child within you. The Controlling Parent may ask the Adaptive Child to come up with some ideas and solutions and ask them to sort the problem out, and the Adaptive Child may think to themselves, 'They are asking me for some solutions – well I don't think so.' In fact these parts of our personality are evoked by the opposite. Thus if I act as an Adaptive Child, I will most likely evoke the Controlling Parent in the person I am speaking to. The nature of transactions is important to understanding communication.

To improve situations where conflict happens, first go to the state that the other person is, in order to talk at the same level; then move yourself and the other person to the Adult level.

Ulterior transactions

Ulterior transactions are when a person communicates at two levels, social and psychological at the same time. The communication seems to be going smoothly on the surface but actually it is a cross-transaction for all practical purposes. This is because even though the ego states are complementing one another (the social level), at the psychological level the contradiction takes place. The psychological level will be conveyed non-verbally, for example, through eye contact, facial expressions and body language, and emotional energy will be expressed through the words people use. Non-verbal language is likely to be key in determining the outcome of the communication.

You need to ensure that your non-verbal language is congruent with your language, your intent and your ego state.

When in Parent mode (standing straight, with head up and looking confident) you could ask to see one of your team members for a meeting and you would say something like: 'I want to see you in my room tomorrow at 10.00 am as I need to have a meeting with you to go through the proposal for next week; remember to be on time and bring the completed documents with you.' The team member might say (in a whiny voice with a slumped posture, head looking down) as they go into child mode: 'I know you want to see me at 10.00 am but is it okay if I come at 11.30 instead please as I really need a bit more time as I have not quite finished them yet?'

Instead of being in a child mode the team member should be in an adult mode and the reply should be in an assertive and strong tone (not aggressive), with a confident posture (ie head held high, shoulders back) before assertively saying: 'I know how important the meeting is and it does need to be held tomorrow; however, I require the morning until 11.30 am to complete the document. If you are free for 11.30 I will definitely be there on time and with the completed documents and we will still have enough time to get the proposal off in the evening post – is the timing ok in your diary?' The response will be 'That's great, thanks for preparing the documents so thoroughly. I'll see you tomorrow morning at 11.30' (Adult).

We are likely to have preferred states or a tendency to adopt some states more than others, and some people have a dominant habitual ego state and find it difficult to behave in any other way. For example: the constant Parent who always criticizes or helps others; the constant Adult who is always rational, unemotional, analytical, preferring facts to feelings; the constant Child who always operates under strong emotions, anger or guilt, looking to indulge themselves, manipulating people and situations and often feeling helpless and dependent.

As a mature person, we need a healthy balance between the three (Parent/Child/Adult). To build relationships and connect with all people you can be particularly influential if you convey some Parent support, some Adult options and some Child warmth. This would then tap into the positive aspects of all ego states of the other person (remember people like people who are like them).

Internal dialogue

The ego states also apply to internal dialogue where your Controlling Parent may tell you not to do something because you won't be good enough (I call these thoughts negative Gremlins). This has come from our early years of childhood and listening to our parents and authoritative figures guiding us. You should realize that these rules no longer serve you well. You can use your Nurturing Parent and your Adult ego state to change your mindset and know you can do whatever you put your mind to.

Key points

At any one time you will have one of the ego states established (often described as your mood), which is dictated by prevailing influences.

You choose which ego state to adopt when you are dealing with someone by the words you use, your tone of voice and the behavioural actions you take.

Your reaction and carefully crafted response to them will bring about change and success.

The ideal line of communication is the mature and rational Adult–Adult relationship and as you remain in the Adult ego state, others will eventually join you.

Summary

Remember you have a choice of how you respond, and choice makes us feel good. When you are in control you can make it work. Do what you need to do, look at it from different perspectives, do it consciously and make active choices.

If you accept that people are different, you can start to communicate differently and match their thinking and receptive styles and stimulate them to achieve better results.

Think of someone you know is difficult. Write down how their approach differs from yours (eg task oriented, people oriented, results driven). Think what you can do to accommodate their traits, knowing that people are all different and look at things differently from each other. Also remember that other people may feel frustrated by your behaviours!

Disagreements will occur sometimes but it's okay to have healthy debate as it often leads to more creativity and better outcomes. However, understanding models like DiSC®, TetraMap® and Transactional Analysis helps us make sense of our own and other people's behaviour and actions and paves the way for controlled and healthy debate rather than conflict. Understanding will also help you to influence and persuade!

Think about the way people interact and behave, and adapt your behavioural style to theirs, remembering you cannot change other people but you can change yourself, even if only for the time you are conversing with them. Remember people like people who are like them! Think about whether they are reacting from a Parent, Adult or Child mode and carefully respond in a way that moves things forwards. Focus on solutions and determine how the other person thinks and what you can do differently to get a more positive outcome.

We can all think situations through differently and clearly in order to have effective working relationships to enable a productive working environment that we are pleased to work in every day. Keeping a solutions-focused mindset will help ease the personal conflict, because it isn't personal, its work.

Managing projects

08

This chapter is for everyone who organizes projects in any format, from small office moves to events for thousands of people. Project management is already a part of the assistant's role in many guises, from one-off projects to regular events you might organize. If a task requires planning, assessing options, organizing activities and resources to deliver a successful result on time and you are accountable to others, then you are already a project manager – even though you may not have an official title or even have had official training. Project management is a key component of what assistants do for their organizations and in their personal lives too.

This chapter will concentrate on the fundamentals of project management, the role of the project manager, understanding project management terminology, and the common problems that can occur and how to avoid them. You can increase your effectiveness as a project manager by knowing the different stages, processes and tools that will give you a good grounding in project management, thus enabling you to actually manage any project with or without technology.

To further your knowledge, you should consult *The Definitive Personal Assistant & Secretarial Handbook*, 2nd edition, which includes information (in Chapter 6) on 'Organizing meetings and events'. And there is a very useful Appendix – a 'Generic checklist for organizing meetings and events', which complements this chapter very well.

Definition and terminology of project management

A definition of a project is: a series of interrelated activities undertaken to achieve specific goals with a timed end result – it has a start, a middle and an end. It usually has a sponsor and a project manager.

Project management techniques and project planning tools are useful for any tasks in which different outcomes are possible – where risks of problems and failures exist – and so require planning and assessing options, and organizing activities and resources to deliver a successful result.

Examples of projects that you may organize are:

- exhibiting at major national exhibitions and conferences;
- running a residential conference or training course;
- moving the office to another location;
- designing new systems and procedures;
- annual general meetings with people attending from different offices and countries;
- many different types of meetings;
- events such as client seminars and conferences;
- team building events;
- voluntary organization's projects such as network for assistants, for example European management assistants;
- charity events;
- and much more including personal events such as weddings and celebrations, whether organized for themselves or the executive they work for.

Below is a glossary of project management terminology that will make it easier to understand this chapter and to understand the terminology when speaking with others who work in project management.

Glossary

Sponsor:	A sponsor is usually part of the senior management team and is ultimately responsible for the project and has the final say on it. Sponsors will have sufficient authority over all parts of the organization that are impacted by the project. They are unlikely to play an active part in the day-to-day management of the project but they will: set the objectives for the project in line with the strategic plan; ensure that appropriate resources are committed; resolve issues where necessary, as well as chairing the project board meetings. They are sometimes known as the 'Project director' or 'Project executive'.
Deliverables:	The expected outcomes over the life of the project – what it is that is going to be delivered.
Milestones:	A milestone is a significant event in a project that occurs at a point in time. The milestone schedule shows only major segments of work; it represents first estimates of time, cost and resources for the project. Milestones are important control points in the project. They should be easy for all project participants to identify.
Project initiation document (PID):	also known as 'Terms of reference' or 'Project charter'. The PID gives a clear path for progression by stating what needs to be achieved, by whom and when and should include success factors/risks and restraints. The PID defines the:

- vision, objectives, scope and deliverables (what has to be achieved);
- stakeholders, roles and responsibilities (who will take part in it);
- resource, financial and quality plans (how they will be achieved);
- work breakdown structure and schedule (when it will be achieved).

Project stakeholders:	Project stakeholders are individuals and organizations who are actively involved in the project, or whose interests may be positively or negatively affected by the project.
Scope:	The project scope sets the stage for developing a project plan for how you are going to run the project. It clearly states the project's objectives and deliverables. The scope definition should be as brief as possible but complete. A poorly defined scope leads to project failure. The development of the scope must involve the project manager, sponsor(s) and beneficiaries.
Work breakdown:	A key project deliverable that organizes the team's work into structure: manageable sections/tasks.

Definition of a project manager and his/her role

A project manager can be defined as: the individual or body with responsibility for managing a project to achieve specific objectives.

Stakeholder analysis

Project managers are accountable for the success of every project they manage and are responsible for identifying the needs, concerns, wants and interests of all the stakeholders. They should conduct a stakeholder analysis of those people who may significantly influence the success of the project. A stakeholder analysis can be used to anticipate the kind of influence, positive or negative, these groups will have on your initiative, develop strategies to get the most effective support possible and reduce any obstacles to successful implementation of your programme.

The final step is to consider the kinds of things that you could do to get stakeholder support and reduce opposition. Consider how you might approach each of the stakeholders. What kind of information will they need? How important is it to involve the stakeholder in the planning process? Are there other groups or individuals that might influence the stakeholder to support your initiative? Record your strategies for obtaining support or reducing obstacles to your project.

Project managers should set themselves up for success by being constantly aware of the following three different activities that run concurrently during any project:

- **Content:** Day-to-day decisions.
- **Structure:** Four stages of the project: definition, planning, execution and delivery/close.
- **Processes:** Management skills.

As the project progresses it is a common mistake to become submerged in the 'content', which is what managers are generally good at, and lose sight of the other two equally important activities – the 'structure' and the 'processes', which could be a huge mistake that could make the project fail.

Content

'Content' refers to the day-to-day decisions that have to be made as the project progresses. This is a key activity and no project would achieve success without it. The content is often the main focus for discussion, either through informal encounters, or through more formal project team meetings.

For example, what would need to be discussed if you were planning to exhibit at a major national conference?

Content discussions would focus on such topics as: Where do you want the stand? What banners do you want on the display? What products do you want to promote? What freebies will you give away? Who will attend? What should they wear? Are they going to use a scan gun? Are they going to advertise in the promotional booklet?

Structure

The life of the project typically passes through four stages: definition, planning, executing and delivery/review/close.

As project managers you need to understand what the stages are and make sure all aspects are covered. You also need to understand that even during the execution stage you may still be required to do some planning if things change or barriers are put in your way. The starting point begins the moment the project is given the go-ahead (for a formal project this is when a contract/scope agreement is signed).

Stage one: definition

Once the project has been conceived, you will need to work closely with your sponsor. Your first task will be to define the scope and purpose of the project. It will help you establish a clear focus on what you have to do and why. You need to establish your project initiation document, identify any major constraints and define the critical success factors for a successful outcome. By the end of this stage you will have established the project's objectives and the project teams are formed (see Chapter 4 on 'Leading effective teams to success'). Responsibilities will be assigned and objectives written, and the initial strategy will be created. This will help you estimate the resources you need to achieve the results identified.

The three steps described below provide a planned approach for collecting the project information necessary for planning, scheduling and controlling the project. These are:

- defining the project scope;
- estimating costs and developing budgets;
- creating the work breakdown structure.

The five steps of project start-up: sequence of events

Step 1: Sponsor initiates the project

The sponsor gives the initial brief and business case to the project manager. The business case will set out how the project fits into the business strategy of the organization, where the project will lead to and the purpose of the project.

Step 2: Strategic investigation

As project manager you then need to understand the brief and business case and make sure that what you are doing is right, minimize any risks or threats and search out any opportunities. You should carry out a strategic 'PESTLE' investigation (Political, Economic, Social, Technological, Legislative and Environmental considerations), which will enable you to understand any restraints on the project.

When applying PESTLE you should look at it from an external as well as an internal point of view. 'Political' could be changes in government and political stability, or who is in what position within the company, their power, vision and goals, or organizational in-house politics. 'Economic' could be the state of the economy, interest rates, exchange rates or salary rates, recession and the cost of living. 'Social' could be cultural aspects, including the population growth rate, division of wealth in society, health and safety, what is and is not acceptable within the culture, working hours, charitable work and so on. 'Technological' could be research and development activity, innovation and recent technological developments, and automation or new technology within the organization. 'Legislative' could be what is happening with changes to legislation that may impact employment, access to materials, resources and imports/exports, or changes to employment law, recruitment, visas and the like. 'Environment' could be the weather, which may affect industries such as tourism and insurance, or the space available within the office, what can or cannot be moved where and so on.

This will enable you to understand any restraints on the project and ensures you do not waste time doing things you should not be doing. It can be used as a prioritizing tool as there may be things you have to do before you can do something else.

To help with this process, the 'PESTLE' can be combined with a 'SWOT' analysis. The 'SWOT' analysis is an important part of the project planning process and is a strategic planning tool used to evaluate the Strengths, Weaknesses, Opportunities and Threats of a project. It involves specifying the objective of the project and identifying the internal and external factors that are favourable and unfavourable to achieving that objective. The strengths and weaknesses usually arise from within an organization, and the opportunities and threats from external sources. See Table 8.1, 'SWOT analysis'.

Step 3: Findings and confirmation

After the research and understanding of the scope and business case, the project manager can then informally go back to the sponsor to explain the findings and agree on any changes they need to make. This stage gives you the opportunity to correct the business case before you commit yourself. You can then confirm that both sponsor and project manager have the same understanding of the project. This will help build trust between the sponsor and the project manager, especially if the sponsor did not expect

TABLE 8.1   SWOT analysis

←————————Helpful————————→←————————Harmful————————→

Strengths (Internal factors)	Weaknesses (Internal factors)
Strengths (Internal factors) How can we use our strengths? What are the attributes of the organization that help achieve the project objective? What strengths can the project team or wider organization bring to the project?	**Weaknesses** (Internal factors) How can we address each weakness? What attributes of the organization might stop achievement of the project objective? What factors within the organization can hinder progress/ success on the project?
Opportunities (External factors) What external conditions might help achieve the project objective? How can we exploit each opportunity? What benefits will be gained from completing the project? What opportunities may present themselves once the project is a success?	**Threats** (External factors) Are there any external conditions that could damage the project? How can we guard against each threat? These may be external factors that we have no control over but need to be aware of.

such thorough strategic research, and the sponsor will feel comfortable with empowering this project to you.

Step 4: Project initiation document (PID)

The project manager then formally prepares the PID (sometimes referred to as 'Terms of Reference' or 'Project charter'). The PID is a guide to the project and clearly lays out its justification, what its objectives will be, and how it will be organized. This is where you bring together all of the information needed to get your project started and communicated to the stakeholders. With a well-defined and detailed PID you can let everyone understand where the project is heading from the outset, answering the questions What? Where? Who? Why? When? and How? The PID is supported by other detailed planning documents that may not be entirely completed by the time that it is prepared. The PID is the outcome of the business case and scope and helps secure funding (if required).

Your organization may have its own template for project initiation documents that you are requested to use.

The PID can be split into three sections:

- project overview, including project scope and business case;
- project approach;
- project approval.

Project overview

Project title and description (identification)

Write a description of what the project is so that all stakeholders can identify the project. Give it a formal name as well as any other terms that might be used to identify the project. If this project is a new incarnation of a previously cancelled or abandoned project, it's a good idea to reference the name of that as well.

Project background and history

Give any background information explaining how the project came about. What is the context of the project?

Project purpose and justification

The project justification describes how and why your project came to be, the business need(s) it addresses (its relevance), the scope of work to be performed or problem to be resolved; how it will affect and be affected by other related activities, and why it is timely. The project justification needs to be clear and precise and show how the project benefits the business. You should derive the project justification from the strategic objectives, for example:

- market demand;
- business need;
- customer request;
- technological advance;
- legal requirement.

If applicable, include details of why existing tools or products are inadequate. If you have supporting documents for any of these reasons, you can list them here and include them as appendices to the PID.

Business case

The business case should have been given to you by the sponsor and you can include it as an appendix in the PID. It describes the effect the project will have on the business and supports this with a detailed account of the risks that should be considered. It may state options and other courses of action that were considered when the project was designed and developed. It should provide a breakdown of project costs and related financing including a cost–benefit analysis, which is used to work out how the costs of the project are balanced against the expected returns – Return on Investment (ROI).

Assumptions

What assumptions are you making at the start of the project? If necessary, schedule time to confirm these assumptions.

Measurable project objectives and goals

This section addresses how the project ties into the organization's strategic goals, and includes the project objectives that support those goals. The objectives need to be measurable.

What specific outcomes will be achieved, and how will you measure these outcomes? The project objectives must address all the work within the project, including cost, schedule and quality measures. Remember to use the 'SMARTER' goal-setting technique, which you will find in *The Definitive Personal Assistant & Secretarial Handbook*, 2nd edition, as a downloadable appendix.

Hard measurable objectives are typically difficult to quantify. Easily measurable objectives have a unit of measure (for example a percentage of change, a specific amount of money or value, a unit of time).

Examples of hard measurable objectives include:

- improve client satisfaction;
- increase product quality;
- improve process flow;
- increase employee productivity;
- improve information flow.

Examples of easy measurable objectives include:

- increase in sales by a defined percentage;
- reduce costs by a defined percentage or specific cost amount;
- reduce product production waste by a defined percentage;
- reduce manufacturing time by a defined period of time on a per unit basis.

A project manager should encourage the sponsor to convert hard measurable objectives to easy measurable objectives; for example, instead of 'increase product quality,' you could say 'reduce defective products by 10 per cent'. Instead of 'increase employee productivity,' you could say 'increase the number of calls handled by each person by 5 per cent, allowing us to handle more calls with the existing staff.'

Project sponsorship and major stakeholders

Name the project sponsor and stakeholders and eventual project owners. In addition, identify the role of each individual listed so that there is no confusion concerning responsibilities later down the line.

Pertinent documents and references

List any related documents or other resources that could be helpful in understanding various aspects of the project, such as the business case, and include them as appendices to the PID.

Product acceptance criteria

The process and criteria for accepting completed products, services, or results.

Constraints

You must take into consideration anything that will influence your deliverables and schedule. Think about which restrictions can limit what you can achieve, how and when you can achieve it, and how much it will cost to achieve it. These are external variables that you cannot control but need to manage.

Project scope and limitations

The scope is one of the most important sections of the PID because if it is not written in detail to begin with, it can be the source of argument later on in the project. It should include what the boundaries are for the project for example, type of work, type of client, type of problem, geographic area covered and so on.

The scope usually has three parts, which are:

● project scope statement;

● in scope;

● out of scope.

Project scope statement

A well-written scope is crucial to a project manager's ability to make intelligent decisions, and the more information you can gather in the early stages of a project the more adaptable you can be if you should have to deal with obstacles that might appear during the project. Scopes outline the results the project will produce and the terms and conditions under which the work will be performed.

Of course predicting the future is impossible, but the scope statement represents your project commitments, based on what you know now and expect to be true in the future. If and when situations change, you have to assess the effect of the changes on all aspects of your project and propose the necessary changes to your sponsor. Your sponsor has the option of either accepting your proposed changes (allowing the project to continue) or cancelling the project.

Your scope statement should include the following information:

- Describe what is 'in scope'
  You will find that the more specific and detailed this section is, the less confusion and argument about the scope there will be later on in the project's life. It should be clearly detailed so that all parties involved are very aware of exactly what the project includes as well as what it doesn't. It is better to write more than less, and you may need to get clarification from the sponsor or at least cover any limitations in the section on what is 'not in the scope', and these can be discussed when you go for sign-off.

  For example, it could say that 'this project is for the Human Resources Department and all other departments are out of scope.' In other words it defines what is relevant to the project you are working on. The people who requested the project and the project key stakeholders should agree to all terms in the scope statement before actual project work begins.

- Describe what is 'out of scope'
  List any areas excluded that you believe stakeholders might assume are included, but are not. It is crucial that you identify work that might fall outside the project scope (ie what you will not be delivering), as well as how the project work might interact with other projects. Identifying the exclusions is important because it enables you to set expectations with your sponsor, project team and stakeholders. The more specific you are, the less opportunity there is for misunderstanding at a later stage in the project.

  Examples of what might not be covered by the scope could be:

  - any upgrades required to other systems to enable them to work with the new system;
  - all advertising and marketing required for launch and on an ongoing basis will not be delivered or paid for by this project;
  - any recruitment required or resources once the new system has been launched.

A comprehensive scope statement is a key document that binds you, your project team, the project sponsor and the customer. It is an agreement that defines the work of the project and the customer's business objectives. A comprehensive scope statement can help you identify changes in scope after the project has started and help you plan for any modifications or adjustments that might be needed during the life of the project.

Project approach

This gives a high-level overview of how and when the project will be completed. There are several standard components that normally comprise this section.

Project deliverables

List what the project will deliver as outputs. Where you can, describe deliverables as tangible items like reports, products or services. Remember to include a date when each deliverable is expected. List the major deliverables of the project and include the milestones and when these goals should be achieved, and remember to monitor the milestones.

Responsibilities and roles

You may feel it appropriate to create a diagram of the project organization structure showing the lines of authority and reporting for each project team member:

- Name the project sponsor who has the ultimate authority and control over the project and its implementation.
- Name the project manager, stating his or her responsibilities.
- Name any other key stakeholders.

Project team members

As the project manager you then identify and select an effective and efficient team (if you have the choice). Remember to look at Chapter 4 on developing teams, stages of team development and Belbin® team roles.

Identify who the key members of the project team are and their roles and job descriptions. Include contact details – phone numbers and e-mail addresses. Set out who they should report to on a daily basis.

List the required skills and expertise that each individual brings to the project as well as each person's responsibilities. You need to be clear about roles so that you don't duplicate responsibilities, but you do need to have back-up so people may have a primary role and a secondary role as a contingency plan. Everyone needs to be clear about what's expected of them.

If this is a long-term project, you may even consider developing job descriptions for team members.

Project resources

In addition to the human resources, what other resources will be needed for satisfactory completion of the project? Provide a list of equipment such as computers, raw materials, working space and any other resources that might be required. If certain resources will only be needed during specific phases of the project, make a note of that as well.

Risk management overview

Risk analysis: identify, assess, manage, monitor, action

Identify the risks within the project; then you will either need to assess them and decide how you will manage, monitor, accept or take action upon them. Describe what you are going to do to manage risks. Where you can't prevent risks, what are your contingency plans for dealing with them and what likely impact will they have on the project? What actions will you take should the risk materialize? What processes do you have in place to routinely assess the risks associated with your project? Are the risks low, medium or high? Low risks are generally ignored, medium risks you have to keep an eye on, and high risks should have contingency plans.

For example, unquantifiable objectives, such as customer satisfaction can involve high risk.

Project's life overview

Give a basic breakdown of the project's life and list the various stages that your project will go through. Make sure to include the objectives of each stage and why the stage is necessary.

Basic project control and communication plan

The project control component explains the tools that will be used to assist the project manager in tracking the project's progress. It also serves as a communication device for communicating the project's progress to the project team, project sponsor and project stakeholders.

Project schedule

Provide a basic schedule overview that lists, among other things, the key milestones and stages of the project. Various documents such as a Gantt chat, including the associated work breakdown structure, should be included. It can be quite advantageous to use a project management software tool to produce a schedule that can be monitored and adjusted as the project progresses, or this can be done on a spreadsheet like Excel.

Project approval

List all of the names and roles of the major stakeholders ready for their signatures, indicating that each of these individuals is satisfied with the details included in the PID.

In addition, if the project will require resources from other departments or groups, a representative from each of these divisions should be listed in the Approval section as well. The signatures of these individuals will signify that they accept their own responsibilities for successful completion of the project and agree to provide needed support.

Step 5: PID sign off

The project manager then formally organizes for the PID to be signed off by the sponsor, the end user/customer (internal or external), stakeholders and themselves, which effectively means that all parties are happy for the project to go ahead.

Stage two: planning

Having established what your project has to deliver and you're clear about what its scope is, you now need to do some planning. Whether your project is big or small, one of the first challenges of project planning is to break the overall deliverable down into manageable chunks to determine the project sequence of activities and time frame. Later, you will use this to work out the schedule, identify the resources you'll need and work out the budget.

Provide information about how the project will be implemented, including timelines and resources. What major tasks (with milestones) will be completed during the project?

Prepare a Gantt chart (see below) or similar schedule of the timeline. Consider how many days' activity will be needed to complete the project. How many support staff will be needed? Will you need to bring more people onto the project team? How will the progress be monitored and communicated? What quality-control procedures will you put in place?

If you have been given a fixed deadline, plan to meet it earlier, and work back from that earlier date. However, err on the side of caution and build some 'cushion'/leeway into each phase of the project. Ambition and aiming high are good attitudes but exercising realism at the outset of a project regarding financials and timescales can save an enormous amount of trouble later.

There may be a number of sub-projects that you will have to coordinate to meet your overall objective. You will need to break down each sub-project and prepare a detailed specification of who does what by when. You will have to agree these details with the team members assigned to carry them out and provide clear direction concerning budgets and other resources.

Work breakdown structure (WBS)

A work breakdown structure provides an opportunity to structure the project in a systematic and logical manner. It is useful for all small and large meetings, events and projects. It is a way of showing, in an easy-to-understand diagram, how the project breaks down into the key and supporting activities. Once you have generated a list of activities and tasks required in order to deliver the project, you can organize them in a hierarchical way where each lower level supports the ones above.

A frequent technique to use is backward planning, so put the end date at the top under the project outcome and work backwards from there. You should take a flip chart (or put several pieces together if it is a large project) or use a whiteboard, and start at the top with the overall project title at the top.

You then use Post-it notes that already have the activities and tasks written on them as this will make it easier to move your ideas around until you have finalized your WBS.

Each main activity is then broken down into its supporting activities, which have to be completed in turn to achieve it. The process is repeated until all the key tasks have been identified. The completed diagram gives an overview of the project and the interrelation of the activities involved.

Having already identified many of the activities it should be easy to sequence them into a systematic structure.

All the work that needs to be done to make the project a success will have been identified. The WBS helps establish the sub-projects that are necessary to meet the overall project objective. It will form the basis of a timed programme of activities, showing the most efficient and economical way forward for the project.

Work breakdown structure example

We will create a new training programme using a WBS.

Brainstorm what major intermediate/final products/deliverables are needed to produce and achieve the project's objectives (for this example these are not exhaustive by any means but are just used to illustrate the WBS structure):

- training programme needs statement;
- training programme design;
- participant workbooks.

Then divide each of these major deliverables into its component deliverables in the same manner. Choose any one of the deliverables to begin with and work your way through each one. For this example I am choosing 'Training programme needs statement'. I need the following intermediate deliverables so I can create the needs statement:

- interviews with potential delegates;
- a review of materials discussing the needs for the programme.

Divide each of these work pieces into its component parts. I choose to start with 'Interviews with potential delegates' for my illustration The deliverables I must have in order to complete these interviews are:

- select interviewees;
- interview questionnaire;
- interview schedule.

I have then taken 'Interview schedule' and broken it down to show just one of its components (ie 'Select interviewees').

Once you get some activities and tasks drilled down, put some dates/deadlines in. A Critical Path Analysis is a diagrammatical representation of what needs to be done and by when. Timescales and costs can be applied to

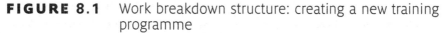

FIGURE 8.1 Work breakdown structure: creating a new training programme

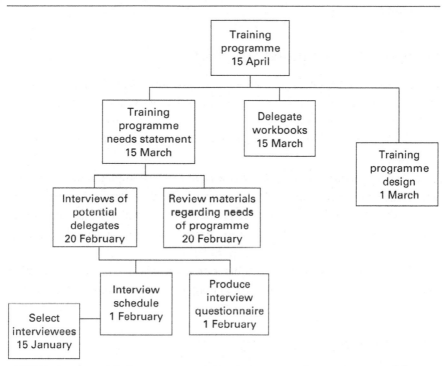

each activity and resource. Look to see where your milestones are. Putting the dates gives it a sense of urgency and you know when you have to have things in place by (Figure 8.1).

The Gantt chart

The Gantt chart (named after Henry Gantt, who developed the procedure in the 1900s) is a useful tool for analysing and planning more complex projects. It helps you to think about people, resources, dates, overlaps and key elements of the project. It allows you to predict the outcomes of time, cost and quantity. When a project is under way, a chart helps you to monitor whether the project is on schedule. If it is not, it allows you to pinpoint the remedial action necessary to put it back on schedule.

Gantt charts can be produced on Excel spreadsheets or you can use software that is simple and easy to use. It is a horizontal bar chart that graphically displays the time relationship of the steps in a project. Each step of a project is represented by a line placed on a chart in the time period when it is to be undertaken. When completed the Gantt chart shows the flow of activities in sequence as well as those that can be underway at the same time.

Sequential and parallel activities

An essential concept behind project planning (and critical path analysis) is that some activities are dependent on other activities being completed first. As a shallow example, it is not a good idea to start running a training workshop before you have designed it, produced workbooks and practised it.

These dependent (sequential)activities need to be completed in a sequence, with each stage being more or less complete before the next activity can begin. Other activities are not dependent on completion of any other tasks. These may be done at any time before or after a particular stage is reached. These are non-dependent (parallel) tasks.

It is well worth your time finding out more about Gantt charts either via the internet or by asking project managers in your office to show you.

Stage three: execute

'If you fail to plan, you plan to fail!' Once you have planned well it is easy to execute your well-defined plans to achieve a successful outcome. You will be involved in monitoring to make sure that the project keeps on target. If the sequence of events is not proceeding to your plan, you will be involved in problem solving and decision making. This often means modifying the project plan in light of new evidence and the response to change. Remember to get the sponsor's approval to any changes in the scope. Be prepared to introduce a contingency plan where appropriate.

Common problems that can occur in project management and how to avoid them

- Scope creep: Recognize that every piece of work you get is a potential project and that people not directly affected by the project will want you to add things to it. Check with the sponsor before proceeding. Make sure you use all the time management tools and techniques in order to hit all the milestones on target. Time management should be a high priority for everyone involved. Scope creep can happen when things change.

- **Poorly defined roles**: Make sure every team member understands who does what and what their role is within the project team.

- **Lack of documentation**: Ensure that all details are written down in the PID and Gantt charts, which should be accessible and visible for all to see, that minutes are written up and all communication channels are open appropriately with all key stakeholders. It is important to keep everything documented, and to keep the documents even after the project is finished in case questions come up later.

- **Over-budget**: Budget with educated estimates rather than 'guesstimates.' Keep an eye on spending or put someone with the appropriate skills in charge.

- **Over-dependency**: As project manager you should make sure that people have cover and that you don't rely too heavily on one person for any particular role. Train people to double up for the different roles.

- **Poor team morale**: Make sure the team is motivated (see Chapter 2). There may be lack of clarity, which can cause confusion and lead to people pulling in different directions, building up unrealistic expectations, and having unnecessary worries and fears. Developing a detailed PID at the initiation of the project can help people understand the what, why, where, when, who and how of the project.

- **Changeable deadlines**: Deadlines are agreed in the project schedule; however, some may be brought forward or delayed for different reasons beyond your control, even if risks have been addressed. Be ready with Plan B and calmly sort out alternatives.

- **Mistakes**: No matter how good the planning, and even with the existence of contingency plans, mistakes will happen as we are human. Good leadership, flexibility, support and team development may be required.

- **Resistance to change**: The nature of the project may be alien to what an organization is usually involved in. This may cause resistance amongst the work force, affording slower than possible activity. In severe cases this may lead to sabotage.

- **Priority changes**: If the project is part of a larger programme there may be a pecking order for each project. The projects may be fighting for a pot of central funds. Even within a project there may be prioritization of resources that can seriously affect key areas, so you have to have contingency plans in place and use flexibility and proactive problem solving skills.

- **Changed objectives**: This will mean different processes, analysis, methodologies, team requirements and sometimes even suppliers. Visibly using and enforcing the scope will help you get a Request for Change signed off by the project sponsor, and helps ensure those eventually paying for the work have a better sense of the impact of later changes on project costs, timescales and the ultimate quality of delivery.

- **Insufficient people** (either of the right number, the right experience or the right capability): You need a good mix of experience, enthusiasm and energy, and must make sure your sponsor is aware of resource issues and the consequences. These might include overrunning time, undermining quality, and probably stress and possibly burning people out.

Stage four: deliver/review/close

This is the stage where the project reaches its close. You will need to check that all that you set out to do has been done. Was the eventual outcome acceptable to all those concerned? Highlight what was successful, as well as areas where you feel you could have performed better. You may need to train the end user on whatever your project has produced. You will need to lead a review on the outcome and overall results.

One of the greatest things about formal processes is that you can look back at lessons learned, which helps us to do an even better job next time.

You will need to produce a written report in which you summarize the results and give recognition to the project team for their achievements, and then it is time to celebrate with the team.

Processes

Whilst the content and structure are happening you also have to take care of the processes. Whether you are leading a large or small project, the process is still the same. The benefits of having processes include saving time that you can use elsewhere in the project. They will reduce errors, allowing you to see what might go wrong, helping you to minimize or avoid it ahead of time. A process is also reliable as you know that when you do something you will get a certain result, allowing you to move on to the next phase. There is a degree of confidence that comes from understanding a process, because as you use a process repeatedly your skills improve and your confidence increases.

If you are currently a team member of a project and you would like to be the project manager one day, then practise these processes regularly, even if it is on a small meeting. You will then be able to transfer your skills into larger more visible projects that you may get involved in. Take the time to learn and do it right.

If you don't have the time to do it right, then when will you have the time to do it over again?

A good process will also help with communication in terms of where you are in the project and understanding what you should be working on next. This makes a big difference to teams working together.

All project managers face problems – efficient and effective project managers are working on next week's or even next month's problems.

Summary

For a project to be successful, it's not enough simply to manage the project competently and deliver a good-quality product on time. To avoid failure, make sure you have identified the right business requirements, created an achievable business case/scope, communicated effectively with all key stake-holders including the project team members on a timely basis, managed a high-quality execution, focused on outcomes and monitored your changing environment. You also need to use excellent people skills to manage your team effectively and build trusting relationships ready for the next project that you are asked to manage.

Importantly, you have to manage the expectations of your sponsor, stakeholders and team members so that they stay supportive and endeavour to take the project to success.

As a final point, with today's digital communication and technological world where people work virtually, information moves fast: we share documents via 'clouds'; we can sign off electronically. You need to keep up to date with technology and be aware of what is available such as Web 2, Enterprise 2.0, MS Project, PMBOK – 'Project Management Body of Knowledge' – PRINCE2. Embrace the change in technology – keep on top of what's new – have fun using it but above all else share information as you never know what you have that could be extremely valuable to others.

The art and science of effective negotiation

09

Negotiation is both an art and a science. It involves the systematic analysis of problems (the science) and the interpersonal skills an individual needs to deal with people (the art). The ability to negotiate is a skill relevant to most areas of our lives. Assistants and leaders in particular will need to negotiate on deadlines and procurement, and deal with colleagues on many issues, such as coming to an agreement on how the business should be run, which tasks should be prioritized or negotiating change management. Effective negotiating will enable you to meet your needs and the needs of others without causing conflict and help you persuade people to help you, over whom you may or may not have direct authority. Virtual assistants will particularly use negotiation skills whilst conducting their business.

This chapter will give you the interpersonal and communication skills as well as practical tools to prepare for the different stages of negotiation. You will understand the different negotiating styles that you can use and the tactics and techniques available to you, including effective and not so effective questioning skills. You will learn how to communicate effectively and pick up on verbal and non-verbal cues from the other party. It will consider information-handling skills, which includes being knowledgeable about all the issues involved and possessing the ability to use that knowledge flexibly and discretionary. Judgmental skills allow you to make decisions on behalf of yourself and your organization using your own discretion. It will enable you to achieve successful win–win outcomes, whether negotiating for the best deals with venues and suppliers, negotiating contracts, engaging in conflict resolution or negotiating with members of your own team, your boss and your colleagues.

When you don't want to do something, consider negotiating instead of saying 'Yes alright then' or 'No I won't do it.' The first is too weak, the second too aggressive. In both cases you'll come out better if you negotiate the deadline.

Most people have a particular negotiating style, and when you learn the tactics you will be able to recognize these in other people and understand how they think, and therefore know how to counteract their obvious and subtle tactics. You will be able to read their body language and use your body language to help you gain successful outcomes.

The skills used in negotiating, such as interpersonal communication, will help in many situations. Ethical influencing – persuading, negotiating and convincing – is the foundation of successful leadership, relationship building and customer service.

Definition of negotiation

Negotiation is simply the act of reaching an agreement through discussion among two or more people with the goal of moving forward where everyone feels satisfied with the outcome. Effective negotiation helps you to resolve situations where what you want conflicts with what someone else wants.

It is a communication between two parties who have different goals.

Negotiation styles

Learning about the different styles that negotiators use and understanding how to use them appropriately will ensure that you approach people in the correct way to achieve a positive outcome. Some people negotiate quickly whilst others take risks, and some take their time and try to avoid risks. Some negotiators can be quite intimidating to the point of being rude whilst others are quite passive and easily manipulated. To negotiate with all these different types, we need to be able to adapt our behaviour and be flexible in our approach.

FIGURE 9.1 Five typical negotiation behaviours

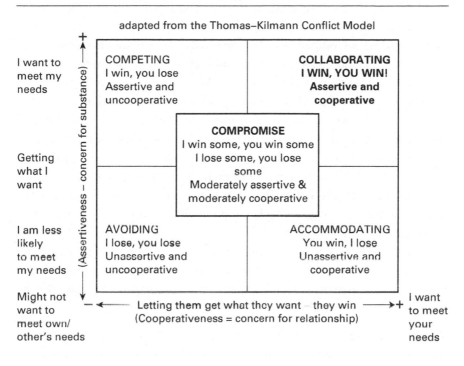

A popular model for explaining the approach to different typical behaviours of negotiation styles is the negotiation model above, which is adapted from the Thomas–Kilmann Conflict Model developed by Kenneth W Thomas and Ralph H Kilmann. They state that there are five different modes for responding to conflict situations – see Figure 9.1: The five different styles are: **Competing** (or Aggressive), **Collaborating** (or Cooperative), **Avoiding**, **Compromise** and **Accommodating** (Conceding). The best negotiators are able to use the different styles and choose the most appropriate one for each type of negotiation.

Competing (I win, you lose)

Competing style negotiators are usually assertive and uncooperative, and some people view negotiation as a game they have to win. They use 'hard' negotiation tactics, which often leaves one party feeling very satisfied and the other side feeling that they have no choice but to agree. The problem with this approach is that the relationship between the two parties is often permanently damaged. The person asking for something may receive it, but the second person probably feels taken advantage of and perhaps angry and resentful. If it was a reluctant agreement, the person who conceded is unlikely to complete the work quickly or with a positive attitude.

When using a Competing style individuals may pursue their own needs at the other person's expense, often using whatever power and tactics they can think of, and they can be aggressive. Whether it's their ability to argue, their status or the fact that the other person is weaker than them, they simply want to win. Competing means standing up for your rights and defending a position you believe in. However, Competitive negotiators may not necessarily or purposefully want to cause suffering (losing) to the other party. It could just be a by-product of their competing behaviour.

Negotiators use this behaviour when they need to get results quickly, but if you are always using this style people will soon learn and not want to negotiate with you.

I recommend that if you are negotiating with a Competing type behaviour person, you should use a blended approach of the different styles as appropriate. A person who prefers this type of negotiating may also be more interested in 'winning' rather than reaching an agreement.

Word of warning: Appeasing Competitive negotiators does not create goodwill as they may perceive you as weak and demand more concessions. Restate your position firmly, using strong language such as 'we need...', 'we require...' etc. Remember never to reward bullies by conceding when you know and feel you shouldn't – remain strong and stand up for your rights.

Accommodating (I lose, you win)

The opposite approach to competing is 'Accommodating', which is unassertive and cooperative. This is when one person or party simply agrees to what the other person wants whilst neglecting their own wants and needs, which means they sacrifice something.

This tactic is often the result of wanting to keep relationships friendly and to avoid conflict. It might mean Accommodating parties have selfless generosity or charity, or they may obey an order when they prefer not to or concede to another person's point of view. The end result, however, is that they lose control to the other person or party. Again this may leave one person/party feeling resentful that they have let themselves down.

The relationship that Accommodating style negotiators have with other people, is very important to them and they believe that the way to win people over is to give them what they want. Accommodators are usually very well liked by their colleagues and opposite party negotiators.

As repairing the relationship is critical to these types of negotiators, if they have nothing else that would benefit the other side after conceding some things then they feel they are in a weak position and believe their best option is to give in gracefully. At this point an Accommodating negotiator should remind the other person/party what they will both stand to lose. If you both intend to work together in the longer term, then refocus the negotiations on the longer term.

Word of warning: It is almost always a bad idea to use the 'Accommodating' style when negotiating against 'Competing' styles as they will take it as a sign of weakness to be taken advantage of. If you always use the Accommodating style you could be perceived as a 'doormat' by others.

Collaborative (I win, you win)

Collaborative (also known as win–win) is both assertive and cooperative. These are negotiations where all parties show respect and concern for everyone's point of view/needs and wants. They aim for mutually satisfying outcomes and are often best for everyone concerned, where everyone is left feeling happy and satisfied. 'Win–win' is where all parties feel they have benefited somehow even though they may have had to find a fair compromise. The main difference is that this style takes time, and collaborative negotiators who are willing to invest time and energy to find innovative solutions to problems, know that they will feel positive about the end result and it will be more valuable.

Collaboration is the best style to use in negotiations as you will need to understand the feelings and deeper interests or motivators of all negotiators. The advantages are that it accomplishes mutual satisfaction for both parties, builds trust, gains commitment and they can continue their relationship.

Many people confuse 'win–win' or the Collaboration style with the Compromising style. However, the Collaboration style is about making sure both parties have their needs met, with as much mutual value created as possible through innovation. Collaborative profile negotiators are adamant that their important needs must be met – and they acknowledge that the other party has needs that must be met too. Compromising is when one or both of you will 'lose' some things.

Collaborative negotiations are based on trust, relationship, and creativity. Your questions need to explore options, build consensus, and test boundaries.

Questions you could ask in the collaborative style are:

- 'Under what circumstance would you consider...'? (powerful question)
- What if...?
- What is your primary issue with...?
- What is your main objective?
- Do you have flexibility with...?

Avoid (I lose, you lose)

Avoiding is unassertive and uncooperative – the opposite of the Collaborative style. People who habitually use this style really dislike conflict and they neither pursue their own concerns nor think about the other person's needs. Rather than talk directly with you about the issue, 'Avoid' styles may try to sidestep it, postponing an issue until a better time or simply withdrawing. The Avoid style can be a typical reaction to the Competing negotiators. You can use the Avoid style when the value of investing time to resolve the conflict outweighs the benefit or when the issue under negotiation is trivial to both parties.

Sometimes there is just not enough at stake to risk a difficult conflict situation and it is sometimes better to allow people to calm down and take a break and resume later when you are feeling more reasonable and rational. At that point an Avoid style is likely to be the most pragmatic alternative.

The Avoid style is useful when you find yourself in a negotiation where you are unprepared; it allows you to either avoid the meeting or avoid discussing the issues until you have had chance to prepare properly.

> One way to use the Avoid style of negotiating is to say: 'If you want an answer from me right now then I will have to say no; if you can wait then it may be a different answer.'

Word of warning: The Avoid style of negotiators are frequently seeking to avoid conflict; however the fact that they have avoided the discussion or meeting may cause the other party to be frustrated and even resentful, which can cause even more conflict than what they were trying to avoid in the first place.

Compromise (I win some, you win some; I lose some, you lose some)

Compromising is moderate in both Assertive and Cooperative behaviours. This style is about finding a solution that can be mutually accepted and partially satisfies both parties. This is what most people think of as a negotiation. Compromising often involves splitting the difference, usually resulting in an end position about halfway between both parties' opening positions. Both parties win and lose – but make sure you win and lose the right things. Meeting halfway can reduce the strain on relationships.

If you are not familiar with negotiation tactics and do not prepare well, then you may bluff your way through the discussions and end up compromising. If the outcome of the negotiation is critical, then you should not compromise on things that you absolutely must have.

Compromising style negotiators give up more than Competitive negotiators, but less than Accommodating negotiators. This style addresses an issue more directly than avoiding but does not explore it in as much depth as Collaborating.

Word of warning: One of the problems with Compromising is: if you make concessions without good reason then the other party may assume that you will make more concessions without the need for a clear and strong rationale. Calculate before the negotiation where you can compromise and the reasons for doing so. Compromises cheat both sides out of innovative solutions so remember to think about using the Collaborative style instead by making it safe to explore options together. Invite the other side to join you in 'what if' scenarios to explore possibilities.

Only compromise when you have a strong rationale for doing so, and when you are receiving something back in return. Stay with the problem or opportunity for longer. Don't give in so easily to the temptation of splitting differences until you've explored other alternatives.

Applying a negotiation style

To apply a negotiation style work through your list of goals and aims, taking into consideration what concessions you decide you could make before the negotiation begins. Decide which issues are best to: Collaborate, Compete, Compromise, Avoid or Accommodate on.

Each of us is capable of using all five styles and some people use some modes more than others. Your negotiating behaviour is a result of both your personality/behavioural style and the requirements of the situation you are in. Be prepared to pause the negotiation and be ready to revert to another style when necessary and appropriate.

The key skills of a negotiator

Your mindset as a negotiator is just as important as the techniques, tactics, tools and soft skills required that are used throughout the negotiation process. Below are some key skills you should learn to be an effective negotiator:

- Remain positive and confident in your skills whilst keeping your desired outcome in mind. Think of a Collaborative or win–win outcome.

- Simply think of negotiations as conversations that you are good at.

- Make sure you are negotiating with the right person/party – many negotiations happen with the wrong person and much time can be wasted.

- Become a trusted negotiator – if you want to have high-level negotiations with high levels of trust it is important to assess character, competence and whether the other side are empowered to make decisions. You have to be able to trust each other.

- Remember you need to maintain effective working relationships after the negotiation has ended. You need to anticipate how people will feel about a proposal you make and how they are likely to react, and you must have the ability to offer concessions without losing sight of your own goals and objectives.

- Master the ability to reinforce the content or meaning of what you are saying with your physical actions, demeanour, intonation and delivery style; this improves the effectiveness of the point you are trying to make.

You need to use influencing and persuasive communication skills so you can get your point across effectively and passionately without raising your voice or letting your emotions take over. You also need excellent active listening skills to be able to understand and glean all the information you need in order to read the other negotiator's body language and not only hear what they are saying but are able to 'read between the lines' and know what they are not saying! Using the right language and body language plays a huge part in effective negotiations. By listening attentively, you show the other party that you respect and value them and that you are interested in their needs.

The stages of a successful negotiation

Stage 1 Before the negotiation   Preparation.

Stage 2 During the negotiation   Opening statement.

Stage 3 During the negotiation   Discussion (including tactics).

Stage 4 During the negotiation   Bargaining.

Stage 5 Agreement and action plan.

Before the negotiation – preparation

When it comes to effective negotiation tactics, thorough and meticulous preparation is key. Not only will you gain the upper hand over the other person/party with the knowledge you acquire, it will also build your confidence, enabling you to gain your desired outcome. Remember a good case does not guarantee a favourable result but a bad case will definitely lead to disaster.

Establish the problem

It is essential to establish and identify what the problem or issue is before you start to negotiate, and to agree on the problem with the other party. Often arguments occur because you and the other person are discussing different issues and it's just a misunderstanding or miscommunication. You should repeat the problem in your own words and ask if it is accurate. You should say things like:

- 'You feel that...'
- 'You are saying that...'

If the other party does not agree with your restatement of the problem then you should ask questions to elicit information about it. You could say:

- 'Can you explain it to me another way (or in more detail) and perhaps give me examples';
- 'How is this problem affecting you?'
- 'How would you like us to solve this problem?'

Once you have identified the problem or issue, then decide on how important it is. Understanding exactly what the issue is and the importance of it allows you to do the basic research.

Information gathering

Information gathering requires research and analytical skills with the ability to draw relevant conclusions and produce documents to support your case. It also includes decision making and discretionary skills as you need to decide on the information you require and what you might disclose to the other party.

For example, if you are negotiating a salary rise, to help your case you may wish to research current market offerings in your industry and geographical area and cost of living expenses, or produce survey results or gather information from recruiting agencies and cut job advertisements out of the newspapers or print them off the internet from such sites as LinkedIn etc. If you find many jobs are paying less than what you are asking for, you would of course withhold this information and only produce those jobs that are offering more.

There are many situations where you will need to gather information before you negotiate and you can do this by research and asking questions.

Questioning skills

Good questions vs bad questions

Can you tell the difference between the various types of negotiation questions? How often can you tell when the other party are using questions in order to get a 'fight or flight' response?

Asking questions the right way is both an art and a science. Ask the question the wrong way and the other person/party might become defensive and withdraw from the negotiation or the question may make them angry. Ask it the right way, and the person might talk so you get all the information you need. We need to learn how to ask questions to get vital information, and we need to think about how to ask questions to get the other party to talk.

Effective/useful questioning skills ('good questions')

To be a successful negotiator, you have to know the wants, needs and motivators of the other party. The easiest, quickest way to uncover this information that you can use to your advantage is through skillful questioning from all possible angles and perspectives. With practice, you will find yourself asking better questions and gaining increasingly valuable information.

You should ask questions to help you to adjust your personal negotiation style to best fit your opponent's psychological tendencies, strengths, weaknesses and objectives; find out their behavioural style; gain their opinion (indicates you are interested in what they have to say); gain information; get the conversation back on track; find out what their goals are and reduce tension.

Types of questions

- **Closed** and restrictive questions where the answer will be brief or with a yes or no reply. This type of question is useful for obtaining a specific piece of information, directing a conversation to a desired area or gaining commitment to a definite position.

- **Open-ended** and expansive questions reveal much more about your counterpart's objectives, needs, current situation and behavioural style. Open-ended questions often start with the words 'What, where, when, why, who and how'; for example 'How did you arrive at that conclusion?' Be careful with the 'why' questions as it may put the other party on the defensive if worded wrongly.

- **Probing** questions, where you dig deeper to find out more information and keeping digging deeper until you get the answer you require.

- **Open-opportunity** questions invite the person to participate and offer their views; for example 'What do you think of this option?'

- **Leading** questions, which are questions where you try to guide the person to your point of view in an influencing and persuasive manner. For example 'With everything I have just said in mind, don't you think it is the best way of working for both of us?'

  Another form of a leading negotiation question is to simply let the question tail off, which invites the other person to fill in the blanks. For example 'After we provide those documents that you asked for, you will...?'

- **Flattery** questions are effective because they are both complimentary and they make the other party feel good. They will therefore respond well and the result is that you can elicit information from them. For example 'As I know you are an expert in delegating and always deliver on time, could you please delegate these smaller pieces of work so that we can concentrate on this bigger piece together?'

- **Emotional sensor** questions – there may be times when you sense that emotions may be rising and at this time it would be a good idea to address a possible issue that might upset the negotiation by simply checking out how the other person feels about certain issues. For example 'How do you feel about what we have discussed so far?'

'Bad' questions

These are types of questions that can be counterproductive to negotiations, being perceived as confrontational and possibly inducing negative emotional responses. The other party may be put on the defensive or your question may cause them to respond aggressively or emotionally, which will in turn bring the negotiations to a close or at least set you back.

- **Aggressive**: Certain kinds of question can result in you appearing to be too pushy, especially when used at the wrong stage of your negotiation. For example: 'You are not trying to bluff your way out of this are you?'

- **Loaded questions**: These carry an assumption and are worded in such a way that the respondent who answers the question admits to accepting that assumption. This style of question puts the person on the hot seat regardless of how they respond, and therefore in a very defensive position. A loaded question is really two questions phrased as one. The loaded question assumes that the first answer must be true; otherwise why would someone phrase it that way? For example: 'I notice that you are on the internet a lot; do you speak on Twitter, LinkedIn and Facebook most of the time?'

- **Emotional trigger questions**: Certain questions may trigger a powerful emotional response, particularly when posed with a hint of arrogance or insult. By using this type of question you will not elicit any information you need and will probably stop the negotiation process. For example: 'Do you think I should waste my time on this ridiculous proposal – it's not been thought about properly has it?'

- **Impulsive question**: Speaking before you think. Always think – then ask, not the other way around.

- **Innuendo questions**: These questions could be perceived in different ways and may even imply a threat. For example: 'Are you in a position to concede on these points now or do you want to take it further?'

It is true that some of these types of questions may elicit the response you want; remember, however, what kind of brand or reputation you want to express and consider whether these questions will get you what you want in a durable and long term way. Think about the consequences and what kind of relationship you will have after the negotiations.

Objectives

You need to identify your objectives and priorities and know at what point you will walk away. Winning at all costs to get the best result rather than reaching a compromise will often bruise egos and make any future negotiations difficult or even impossible.

Most negotiators have three basic positions when they are in talks. Decide on what your ideal and best outcome is, your realistic and satisfactory outcome, and your acceptable minimum bottom line – ie your fallback position, the one you can live with.

The negotiation itself is a careful exploration of your position and the other person's position, with the goal of finding a mutually acceptable compromise that gives you both as much of what you want as possible.

Expected outcomes

What outcome will people be expecting from this negotiation? What has the outcome been in the past, and what precedents have been set? Clearly structure the outcome desired by both parties by writing it down (see Resource 7, which can be downloaded from **www.suefrance.com** before you do this), consider what you need (the essentials) and what you want (the desirables). Think about and understand what will happen if you cannot reach an agreement. Brainstorming possible outcomes could lead you to solutions that you had not even considered before. Be clear on what you won't compromise on and what your 'walk away' strategy is.

Team negotiations

Consider whether this will be a team negotiation, and if so consider who should be the participants. How the two sides populate their teams will usually have an impact on the outcome. Among other things you should try to keep people out of the negotiation who tend to inflame the situation. If you are negotiating in teams then you should also research the participants of the other team and understand who and what you are up against, why they were included and what role within the negotiating team they are likely to play. Understanding the other team's individual profiles and why they were selected gives an indication of the areas their team leader feels are important or the areas they feel require some expertise.

Facts or assumptions

When preparing, separate the facts from assumptions by understanding what you know about the situation and what you assume to be true. Validate your facts and make sure your information is current. Assumptions need to be tested, validated or discarded. Incorrect assumptions can damage an otherwise possible successful negotiating strategy. Don't set yourself up for failure by relying on an invalidated assumption because you like it or it helps your case.

During the negotiation ensure everyone is aware of the issues to be discussed and uncover any new issue that needs to be addressed. If new information is provided or the issues change, then it is advisable to take a break to reflect or regroup with your team if necessary.

Make sure you have a plan to deal with the outcome whether you win or lose for both short and long-term benefits. As a negotiator, you will want to make sure what you are saying is the best way to get across the intent and that you are being heard. The best way to do this is to practise.

Relationships

Clarify the relationship – what is the current real and perceived business and personal relationship, and what is its true value to your and your organization's future? You must cautiously determine what could be lost in any negotiation and at the same time keep the goal in mind. Think about the history of the relationship. Could or should this history impact the negotiation? Will there be any hidden issues that may influence the negotiation? How will you handle these? Think about the consequences of winning or losing this negotiation – both for you and the other person.

Consider who has what power in the relationship. Who controls the resources? Who stands to lose the most if agreement isn't reached? What power does the other person have to deliver what you hope for? You may need to build relationships with key people before the negotiations – people who can help you with your information gathering.

If you are negotiating on behalf of someone else, you may need to get their agreement on what you have planned. At this stage you will need to have clarity, be assertive, capable and have influencing and persuasive skills to put your case forward both for the agreement and for the negotiation itself.

Values and beliefs

Values and beliefs determine how you and the other party view the world and how you prioritize your life, decisions and actions. The other party's beliefs can also present fears, anxieties and concerns that you can use to your advantage throughout the negotiation process. Your goal is to dissect these value and belief patterns, determine the influence they have over the other party's decision-making ability and develop an appropriate strategy on how to use this information to your advantage throughout the negotiation process.

Pre-negotiation tactics

A pre-negotiation tactic could include an informal meeting to elicit information; using the grapevine, but better still your own ears and eyes (but be aware of wrong information from third parties); using the devil's advocate and looking at it from a neutral position and projecting yourself in the opponent's position. You will then have further information to be able to predict counter-claims and schemes by the other party; consider possible concessions of both parties and thereby be prepared to respond to arguments and better able to decide on a 'fall-back' position.

Determine the ideal location for the negotiation, which should not be held in the other party's office as that gives them psychological power. Factors that you should consider when setting up an effective location for the negotiation include room location, time of meeting, layout of chairs and tables and so on.

During the negotiation – opening statements

The first few seconds

When meeting the other person/party, you should seek to create the desired impression right from the start. (Read Chapter 1 on 'Building relationships' in *The Definitive Personal Assistant & Secretarial Handbook*, 2nd edition).

Agenda

Set and agree an agenda to keep the meeting structured, the dialogue focused and moving forward to a win–win conclusion.

Hidden agendas

People can have hidden agendas, which are the personal and private goals and objectives that affect the way we negotiate. Hidden agendas are likely to be different for each person and even for co-negotiators on your own team.

To uncover hidden agendas:

- Ask questions to get the other person's needs and wants, and then ask follow-up questions designed to cross-check or validate previous answers. Question the responses if you feel it necessary as it is important to understand not only the words being used but the meaning behind them so you truly understand the message of what you are being told.

- Make sure the message and the non-verbal body language, gestures and facial expression are congruent with each other; if they are not, ask more questions.

Who goes first?

If you open first, then you are showing a lead and forcing the other person to follow. If you put a good case, then you may make it more difficult for them, forcing them to try to counter your early initiative. Ask for more than you really want and more than you expect to get – if you don't ask you don't get and you won't know unless you try. If you start high you can always come down but if you start low you have nowhere to go! Having said that, be careful of pitching too high and not allowing the other party to move – this may happen if a principle is at stake. This is your judgement call!

State your case and your needs and make it clear what you want from the other person.

If you open second, then you have the opportunity to respond to whatever the other person says. If you are smarter, you may upstage them.

Listen to their case

In a negotiation, information really is power. There are many reasons to actively listen in a negotiation. The first stage is to listen without interrupting as that shows respect, and your interest will get the other party to give you more information. You can 'pause' them to paraphrase back what you have heard and you can ask them for clarification, but keep these interruptions to a minimum. This can be difficult especially when you are longing to respond to some of the things they are saying. However if you plunge straight into a debate, you may miss some very useful information.

Then probe for understanding

When they have made their case, you can then ask deeper questions to probe for further information. If they have left out areas that you might have expected them to cover, it may be because they are not comfortable talking about this. Sustain a gentle approach of interest, curiosity and general inquiry. If you make it sound like an inquisition, they may well stop talking. Your goal is to make it easy for them to tell you more about their situation.

When your proposal or offer is countered, you have the following options: you can accept, reject, or counter back, sit back and do nothing, or ask for a break to consider the terms.

You may find you have to re-evaluate your position and be creative to find solutions. Experienced negotiators read the signals from the other party quickly and accurately. Instead of just giving in you can try trading: 'If you could do this for me then I could do your task quicker and be able to spend a bit more time on what you are asking me to do.'

Separate the people from the problem

If you were to meet these people in a social setting they would probably be entirely different, so concentrate on their behaviours not their personality.

Discussion (including tactics)

Make sure that you share information at the same level of detail and do not give too much, or you could be exploited. There is a balance to get right – you can't give too little as this may stop the negotiations.

If you know in advance of a demand that you are willing to concede, link it to an issue where you require movement from the other party and also remember the Law of Reciprocation. If you concede something they will feel obliged to concede something also. However, you have to remember that giving away too much too early can leave you with a poor hand to play in the rest of the negotiation, and it could signal to the other party that your 'gift' (a concession that they have not had to work for) is just a taster of bigger and better things to come!

Similarly, if the other party offers you a 'gift' be cautious, as they may be trying to lure you into reciprocation, obliging you to give back something of greater value in return. So keep in mind the value of the item being given and the relative value to both sides.

You can proactively vary your emotions from 'stunned' to 'relaxed' depending on the context of the situation. You can make the 'unimportant issues' essential, then concede them at a later time with hesitation, making the other party believe they won a big battle and leaving them feeling satisfied.

Make logical arguments

Intelligent people will not be easily convinced by the use of emotional persuasive tactics. However, if you present them with a logical argument that breaks down your point of view into facts, statistics, business plan and data that they cannot disprove, then you will effectively win them over to your way of thinking.

Words are a critical component of the communication process. Sometimes they are so very important, that a few ill-thought-out words can spell your doom and break down the negotiation at a moment's notice.

Here are a few words that have negative or weak connotations and that you should refrain from using throughout the negotiation process as they could possibly ruin your chances of attaining a favourable outcome.

- 'If...'
- 'Hope...'
- 'Can't...'
- 'Try...'
- 'But...'
- 'Should...'

Develop and maintain rapport

Your next objective is to first develop and later maintain a strong rapport with your opponent. This is done in several ways involving the process of mirroring and matching, by observing the other party, carefully, taking notice of their facial gestures, body language and the verbal language they persistently use. Match and mirror their body language and language in order to build relationships at a deeper level. You can even match their breathing to help build rapport.

Match beliefs, values and habits

You can match the beliefs, values and habits that make up their personality, characteristics and behaviours. In order to connect with them at a deeper level, you must show that you are 'like them' in at least some ways. Consciously matching their beliefs and values will show the other party that you stand by the same principles that they believe in.

Acknowledge your understanding as they speak by nodding your head and making short verbal remarks. If they see that you are willingly considering their side of the story, then they will be more open and accepting of your perspective. Be clear that you are only nodding to show understanding of their point of view – not to agree with them.

Think in solution-oriented ways using 'chunking up' and 'chunking down'.

'Chunk up'

When you can't see eye-to-eye with the other party and you begin to feel that problems are getting in the way of your negotiations, decide to 'chunk up' (get to the bigger picture) by seeking common global interests that you and the other party share. These interests will help you establish areas of common ground that you can agree upon and therefore work from in order to reach a favourable outcome. A 'chunking up' question would be: 'How does this fit into the plan we've been following?'

An example of 'chunking up' would be when one person wants to buy cheaper copier paper and the other person thinks it would give a poor impression to the clients. You could ask: 'What would cheaper paper get for us?' and 'What would a good customer impression get for us?' The answers might be 'cost savings' and 'more sales', respectively. One more 'chunk up' by asking 'What do "cost savings" and "more sales" mean to us and our company?' and the answer would be 'We would make more profit.' Then both parties can address the problem with a common goal.

'Chunk down'

When you can't see eye-to-eye with the other party and you begin to feel that problems are getting in the way of your negotiations, decide to 'chunk down', seeking common agreement in the detail that you and the other party share. You may not see the same solution, but there may very well be certain aspects of this solution that you both acknowledge and can agree upon. Identify these aspects and work on re-establishing rapport and finding common ground. A 'chunking down' question would be: 'How does this affect the way I report my work?' taking you down to a particular detail. To chunk down further you may ask 'What are examples of this... ?'; 'What Specifically... ?' or 'What else... ?'

Delaying tactics in order to build tension

Deferred response – get the other party to repeat what they have asked for and then compare the first and second statements. If there is a discrepancy between the two, you can say 'I am sorry I don't quite understand...'

Using time as a negotiation tactic

Time is a valuable commodity to us all and is often overlooked as a tactic that can be used in negotiations.

You can extend the time originally allocated in order to settle or force a resolution. If the issue is a minor irritant for the other party, being openly willing to take more time in order to make an agreement may motivate the other party to agree/concede/settle rather than waste additional time negotiating.

You can shorten the time allowed to come to an agreement. If the issue is a minor irritant for you, being openly willing to walk away leaving the matter unsettled may motivate the other party to settle rather than risk losing the opportunity. This is especially effective if you have other options and the other party does not.

Silence as a negotiating tactic

Imagine that everyone is gathered around a table, the stakes are high, tension fills the air as the other person lays out a detailed counter-proposal for your consideration. Everyone is waiting for your reaction, expecting a response.

Doing nothing causes a 'void' of silence. Often the other person will feel compelled to fill the void. Your silence is sending the message that you are not entirely happy with the proposal. If the other person offers to improve or modify the proposal or if they become otherwise uncomfortable with the silence, they may signal that they have the room to negotiate further. Negotiation necessitates that you have the patience and confidence to be still. If the other party perpetuates a long silence then you should simply wait and let them break it.

Don't rush the negotiation process

Sometimes we rush negotiations too quickly and we fail to identify potential opportunities for agreement that could benefit all parties involved. In such instances it is better to walk away from the negotiation to gather your thoughts, and then step back into the negotiation at a later time with more clarity and 'ammunition' that will help you attain a favourable outcome.

Face-to-face negotiating behaviours that should be avoided by ethical and effective negotiators:

- unclear proposals;
- too many points in their arguments;
- attacking and defending.

Face-to-face negotiating behaviours that should be used by ethical and effective negotiators:

- asking questions;
- building on other's ideas;
- expressing feelings;
- testing understanding;
- summarizing.

Bargaining

Past bargaining can determine the issues for future bargaining but if no precedent exists then power decides. Bargaining should be fair and once an offer is made it should not be withdrawn unless it was clearly stated when negotiated that it is only a provisional measure. Information given in confidence should not be used publicly.

Know what your 'best alternative to a negotiated agreement' (BATNA) is and write it down. This is not your bottom line but an alternative course of action you can take in case you cannot come to an agreement in your negotiations. It gives you more power because you do have an alternative and therefore greater flexibility and more room for innovation than if you have only a predetermined bottom line. You would then know the consequences of what happens if an agreement cannot be reached (it's like a safety net) and you know that you are able to walk away from the negotiation, which gives you more power when negotiating.

Tactical ways of saying 'no'

Instead of saying 'no' you could say:

- 'I'll see what I can do.'
- 'Maybe.'
- 'I'll ask.'
- 'I'll find out.'
- 'I need to ask my boss as s/he has more authority than me.'

Knowing your 'walk away' point

Do not negotiate if there are unrealistic demands being made at any stage as you must avoid having to concede substantial amounts unnecessarily. Walking away avoids raising false hopes that would make it difficult to satisfy later, and by not negotiating under these circumstances you will stamp your personal authority and professionalism on the situation. You should simply give a clear and honest 'I cannot agree to these terms', stating a suitable explanation and reasons with empathy for the other person's situation.

Let the other party know that you mean what you say but are still leaving the door open for them to reopen the discussion if they wish to concede on your 'walk away' issue. It is important to never re-evaluate your 'walk away' during the negotiation.

If new information is presented at this point, take a break to consider the information and take time to process it. It is easy to convince yourself to change your 'walk away' position if you can see that the negotiation will not come to a suitable conclusion for anyone. Remember, the reason for developing 'walk away' positions before the negotiation was to prevent you from being pressured into conceding on critical issues.

This is an instance where, unless the other party reconsiders, you will be far better served strategically in the future by looking for another way of accomplishing your goal, or indeed possibly building new relationships.

Tactic to get closure

If there is only one problem standing between failure and agreement and you are able to make a concession, then make it as long as it is a minor one and doesn't compromise your position. If there are two problems, maybe you could both agree to compromise.

Timing is important when reaching an agreement, as the time to conclude is when there is a collaborative not a confrontational atmosphere.

Agreement and action plan

The art of negotiating is most required when you are presented with an offer that is acceptable. The dilemma is in knowing whether it is the best you can do and whether it is time to stop negotiating and accept the terms.

Some people feel they have to win every deal and every point, which is not a good way to negotiate. If you want to develop relationships and come up with creative solutions then you must understand that you may need to be prepared to lose some battles to win the war.

Holding out for a lost cause is not only against your best interest but also makes you seem stubborn and foolish. Know when to give in on a point and, if it is not a 'walk away' issue and you know what you have previously decided you can concede, then concede graciously and continue to negotiate.

At the end of negotiation find ways to make the other person feel good about something. For example compliment the other person's performance, professionalism or knowledge. Indicate your appreciation that the other person was personally involved in working things out. Ease back from the transaction discussion to a more personal level of conversation.

Indicate that you appreciate how the other person was able to be flexible and help solve the situation. Indicate that he or she has won some loyalty on your part. Try to give the other person a reason to be pleased with more than just the terms of the agreement.

Once you have reached an agreement it is time to evaluate how the process has worked. If you have only achieved some of your objectives try to set a date to review what has been agreed and revisit outstanding points. In any negotiation you want to reach a deal that is acceptable to all involved. When you master the art of negotiation a relationship can be enhanced by the experience.

Unless what has been agreed is immediately summarized and noted, the two parties may leave the discussions with different interpretations of what their agreement really means. The final note taking and summary is therefore a vital part of every negotiation. The final agreement should include all necessary points for implementation, be clearly understood and should not be expressed in ambiguous terms.

Make the final agreement public and put the action plan in writing with both parties signing it. If implementation is to be gradual then specific time limits should be agreed and follow-up meetings may be required to monitor the progress.

Finally, good relations between all parties have hopefully been maintained and the negotiators have ended on friendly terms.

Summary

To be an effective negotiator you have to be able to think of all possible outcomes for yourself and the other party. The other party has to be able to trust you and if you are always calm it translates across all cultures creating clarity and credibility. You need to be in control of your language and tone of voice thereby keeping your reputation intact. You need to be able to develop durable agreements with creative solutions. You need to be likeable because if the other party can't help but like you it has an impact on them and on the negotiations.

When you are asking questions to get information you need to evaluate the circumstances of your negotiation – you want the other party to work with you and not against you. It is important to think about how to best use your communication skills to get the right results. The manner in which you ask your questions can have a powerful bearing on the results of your negotiation so remember to 'think before you speak.'

Negotiation is complex and uses many skills requiring discipline, patience, and an understanding of yourself, the other party as well as the subject matter and the circumstances of your negotiation. It is a gentle balancing act that must be carefully planned from before the negotiation starts to allow both parties to walk away with a win–win agreement.

Great leaders are great negotiators and now that you are an effective negotiator you should be able to recognize situations where negotiating could help you in your leadership role. Maybe it will enable you to lead discussions; negotiate teamwork, avoid conflict or you could negotiate hiring an assistant so that you can reduce your workload. This might even be the time to renegotiate your job description and redefine your roles and responsibilities within the organization. Remember: if you don't ask you don't get and practice makes perfect!

10

Change management: how can you help?

We all demand better, faster, cheaper products and services. Competition is fierce for everyone; a turbulent economy and massive continual technological advances, together with the exciting possibilities of social media, all help to increase the pressure to do more with less. Leaders have to constantly redefine their business strategies and goals, and objectives have to be met. Whether you lead business strategies or help your boss to lead business strategies, it is important to understand the process of change and help to implement it as smoothly as you can.

Success depends on being resilient, positive and engaged while this rapid and accelerating change constantly turns our world upside down. This chapter is about explaining what exactly 'change management' is and how can you help it happen for yourself, your boss and your organization in a productive and less stressful way. It will help you change your limiting beliefs to empowering positive beliefs to enable you to accept change and achieve the best possible outcome for yourselves and others. You will learn how to use empowering questions to foster positivity and get rid of negativity for yourself and your teams.

The chapter will help you think what you can do and say to help yourself and others through an effective and smooth change process, which leads to being more in control and calm and accepting, and therefore more motivated and successful. It will give you ideas on how to be a leader of change whether it is actually your project or not. You will learn theories of change management and what change acceptance means, whilst understanding the emotions of change that people can go through at each stage. It emphasizes that, after change, something better comes out of it and our understanding and positive attitude towards change will help us get there much quicker and with much less pain! The whole process of change can be perceived as an exciting opportunity instead of something to dread or shy away from. This chapter will help you understand and adopt that perception.

What exactly is 'change management' and how can you help it happen effectively?

Change management is...

an adjective:	'My change management skills are improving.'
a verb:	'We really need to change manage that process.'
a noun:	'Change management is key to the project.'

Change management is a structured approach for ensuring that changes are thoroughly and smoothly implemented, and that the lasting benefits of change are achieved.

The focus is particularly on people and how they, as individuals and teams, move from the current situation to the new one. The change in question could range from a simple process change to major changes in policies and procedures as well as mergers and acquisitions that are sometimes needed if the organization is to achieve its highest potential, and sometimes indeed survive!

Change does not happen in isolation – it impacts the whole organization (system) around it, and all the people touched by it.

Change your view of change

When we think of change it quite often makes us fearful, negative, alone, apprehensive and in a state of stress as we wonder what is going to happen. If we could change our view of change and always think of it as something exciting that will stretch our minds and offer new opportunities, we will start to view it as something that can 'open doors' for us. Be full of optimism and enthusiasm and think of it as a challenge and therefore motivating and satisfying; life would be much more hopeful, positive, happier and less stressful. So here is how we are going to do it!

Change your beliefs – become a change optimist!

Through extensive research, Ariane de Bonvoisin (author, entrepreneur and an expert on change) has created the nine 'Principles of change', that really work and that seem to be true of all people who are good at navigating the twists and turns of life. Use them, and you will be on the path to becoming a change optimist, one who understands that from even the most difficult change, something good will come (it always does!). Read the nine Principles below and think about which ones apply to you and which ones you will endeavour to use more fully!

People who successfully navigate change...

Principle 1: Have positive beliefs.

Principle 2: Know that change always brings something positive into their lives.

Principle 3: Know they are resilient, strong and capable of getting through anything.

Principle 4: Know that every challenging emotion they feel is not going to stop them and will guide them to positive emotions that help them feel better.

Principle 5: Know that the quicker they accept the change, the less pain and hardship they will feel.

Principle 6: Use empowering questions and words, think better thoughts, and express their feelings.

Principle 7: Know they are connected to something bigger than themselves.

Principle 8: Are not alone. They surround themselves with positive people who can help, who have the right belief and skills. They create an environment that supports their change.

Principle 9: Take action. They have a plan and know how to take care of themselves.

We can help the change process by changing attitudes from avoidance to acceptance and from resistance to resilience. The ability to deal with change is at the heart of what it is to thrive as a species; as Charles Darwin put it: 'It is not the strongest of the species that survive, or the most intelligent, but the ones most responsive to change.'

When change is introduced, each employee's filter of the world, their past experiences, values and belief systems will produce a different perception and attitude towards that change. You cannot see or measure attitudes but you can see and measure the response towards change:

For example:

- Instead of thinking 'Why is this happening to me?' think 'What new opportunities will this provide?'

- Instead of thinking 'How will this affect me?' think 'What problems will this solve?'

- Instead of thinking 'We have always done it this way,' think 'There could be a better way – what would it look like?'

- Instead of thinking 'Who is doing this to us?' think 'How can I help make this process to manage change easier for myself and everyone?'

Feelings are contagious – when someone around you is feeling negative, it can make you feel negative. Similarly, when someone is positive and passionate about something, it can have an inspiring effect motivating everyone else to be positive and passionate. Change management should consist of making it enticing, exciting and perceived as an opportunity so that others want to be a part of it. When you feel ownership of change and feel a part of it, your attitude will improve.

Reluctance to change the way we do things has always been part of our nature. As Leo Tolstoy reminds us: 'Everyone thinks of changing the world, but no one thinks of changing himself.' It is much easier to reorganize other people than change your own behaviour.

Our reactions to 'being changed' also depend on what the change is. If we really want to change, we will only struggle with the practical difficulties it causes.

Change a limiting belief – NLP technique

This is a neuro-linguistic programming technique that creates an empowering belief using submodality differences between a useful and less useful belief.[1] It will help you stop your limiting beliefs from becoming self-fulfilling prophecies. Remember you have full control of choosing which beliefs you want to retain. The example below is about changing a limiting belief to an empowering and positive one, but the approach has many other applications.

Visual submodalities

For example, think of a picture about a situation or limiting belief that you have. Then, if you currently think of the picture in black and white, change it to a colour picture; if you think of it as dull then change it to a bright picture; if you think of it as near then think of it as far away and so on.

It's simply a matter of changing how you see the picture right now to make it different. If it's a picture of something you would rather get rid of, then make it duller or further away; if it is a belief you want to enhance then make it brighter, nearer, more colourful and so on. You can vary the size of each image; its positions/locations in your mental space (mind's eye) – left, right, top, bottom; the change may involve movement – for example whether it is still, a slideshow, video, movie, looping; it may be two or three-dimensional; framed or unframed; convex or concave; shape – clear/fuzzy/any specific shape to it; style – picture, painting, photo, poster, drawing, 'real life'.

Auditory submodalities

With sounds you can change the volume to either loud or soft, or coming from a particular direction; mono or stereo; clear or fuzzy noise; pitch low or high; fading in and out; voice – whose and how many; other background sounds.

Kinaesthetic submodalities

How you felt/feel; is there a texture to it; sensation; pressure; temperature?

Use empowering questions to change beliefs – NLP technique

There is a lot in NLP about how you use language, and one of the most powerful areas is how to ask questions of yourself and others; for example, 'What is the one thing I can change about my thinking that will give me the best benefit right now?'

Ask yourself (and others) questions with the appropriate structure and voice tone, as that can help change our state and focus. While questions have an impact on us in different ways, consider the different internal impact of asking:

Why does this sort of thing always happen to me?

What can I learn from this so it will never happen to me again?

One leads us to focus on negative states and strategies that haven't worked, while the other leads us to focus on empowering states and strategies that have worked. You can use questions to improve parts of your life, and the impact of asking these type of questions repeatedly is likely to significantly affect how you feel and what you achieve.

Here are some examples of questions you could think about. In this technique we're using good empowering questions to direct attention towards useful states, resources and actions.

What can I do to help others succeed?

What am I going to do to enjoy my day today?

What is the most useful thing I can do right now?

What do I need to do to get better at [specific area]?

What is the most effective way I can move forward?

What is going to be the most fun and going to move me forward today?

What am I going to start doing today, which in starting will help me succeed?

What am I going to stop doing today, which in stopping will help me succeed?

What am I going to continue doing today, which in continuing will help me succeed?

What is [name the person] doing so that s/he achieves things and how can I replicate it?

How good do I want to be at this, how can I get there in the quickest and most fun way?

How can I become more passionate about helping others to succeed?

How am I going to enjoy improving what I do?

How can I achieve more with less effort?

Who can help me with this?

You will be able to think of many more positive empowering questions that suit your situation. Write them down and ask yourself several questions every day – remember to leave a pause after each question to let the question resonate throughout your mind and body. Keep revising these questions every two weeks or so. You will also find some questions to think about in Resource 4, 'Coaching questions'.

A tip on self-talk

Add short phrases at the end of negative self-talk to change your mindset. Try saying it in different tones of voice and see what works for you.

For example add the phrase: 'well for this second it might be true but not anymore.' Therefore if you say 'I am a complete fool,' it will become 'I am a complete fool, well for this second it might be true but not anymore!'

Leading change

Martin Luther King did not simply say, 'I have a very good plan,' he shouted,

I have a dream!

It is imperative as a leader to provide passion and a strong sense of purpose if you want to aid change through an effective transition.

Today's business world is highly competitive and to survive is to reshape to the needs of a rapidly changing world. Customers and clients are not only demanding excellent service, they are also demanding more. If you do not supply it, your competitors will.

Bill Lucas (author and speaker) suggests if you are leading change in your organization you should:

- make connections to the experiences of those with whom you are working so that you can build on a shared past;
- take time to make the case, dealing with difficult issues openly and acknowledging the feelings of those involved;
- actively engage people in creating the future;
- provide a compelling alternative vision and show how it is the best course of action;

- be a role model for the change you would like to see, so that people can see you walking the talk;
- minimize uncertainty and, once you have allowed enough time for reflection, take action.

Although each individual will have different and personal responses to change, people often show their attachment to the team and the way teams bond by joining in a uniform response and the majority way of thinking ('group think'). Although each person in that group might want to do something different, the need to belong to a group is strong and often sways individuals to follow the rest of the team. Therefore our response towards change is sometimes influenced by personal history and sometimes by the social situation.

When you are defining your change management objectives and activities, it's very important to coordinate closely with the wider team – the other stakeholders such as project managers, executive managers and the HR department. Find out who is responsible for identifying change agents and organizing the training and development plan etc.

Once you have considered the change management objectives, you will also need to consider the specific tasks. It is a question of working out what will best help you meet the change management challenge and how to work alongside other people and their projects' activities and responsibilities.

It's important that change should cause as little disruption to the business as possible. This means your staff should be prepared for it. If concerns are ignored or mismanaged, staff will feel vulnerable and demotivated and the quality of their work may suffer.

Change and emotions

People get comfortable performing tasks and processes in a particular way. They are within their 'comfort zone', and you often hear people say 'but we always do it this way.' This comfort provides people with the security of feeling that they are in control of their environment. They know what they are doing and it's human nature to want to stay within our comfort zone, which is why many people's first reaction to change is to resist it. Some of the things that cause them to fear change include: a dislike of a disruption in their lives; they don't want to look foolish if they cannot grasp the new procedure or new ways of working; their jobs may become harder, at least for a little while until they get used to them; and there is a feeling of loss of control. In some cases there may be a fear of redundancy too.

The Japanese have a term called *Kaizen*, which means continual improvement. It is a never-ending quest to be better, and you become better by changing. Standing still allows your competitors to get ahead of you and could be the start of a possible demise.

Theories of change management

There are many theories to help us through change, and one of the most important ones that I would like to bring to your attention is the 'Change curve', which explains explicitly the emotions people go through at four different stages of the change process. Understanding this process is extremely useful for everyone. It shows that, whatever emotions you are going through at the different stages, you will come out the other end accepting, happy and sometimes even delighted. Even if people are made redundant you often hear them say 'It's the best thing that ever happened to me – the job I've got now is much better than the last one and it suits my needs more.'

Understand the emotions of change using the 'Change curve'

Ensure that people involved and affected by the change understand the change process and have access to help and support during times of uncertainty and upheaval. Assess the training needs driven by the change, and plan when and how these will be implemented. Identify and agree the success indicators for change, and ensure they are regularly measured and reported on.

The Change curve model attributed to psychiatrist Elisabeth Kubler-Ross, resulting from her work on personal transition in grief and bereavement, is a popular and powerful model used to understand how people will react at the different stages of change. Understanding this helps you to get through change easier and helps you to help others by making sure they have the help and support they need.

The model describes the four stages most people go through as they adjust to change.

Stage 1: Change is first introduced

People's initial reaction may be shock or denial. Once the reality of the change starts to hit, people tend to react negatively. Even if the change has been well planned and you understand what is happening, this is when the reality hits and people need to take time to adjust. People need information, need to understand what is happening, and need to know how to get help. It is critical that they are communicated to often and at the same time make sure that this doesn't overwhelm people: they'll only be able to take in a limited amount of information at a time. But make sure that people know where to go for more information if they need it and ensure that you take the time to answer any questions that come up.

If you ask people's opinions they will feel involved. Engaging people in dialogue rather than simply telling them what is going to happen ensures that information is shared. It also encourages people to be creative and to possibly come up with solutions that may have not been thought of, especially ones related to their own area that they work in. They know it better than anyone else. Such dialogue sends out strong messages about the respect you have for them and provides space where feelings can be shared.

We all like certainty and knowing where we stand. Much of the resistance to change may be due to a lack of clarity. The role of the leader is to offer a clear vision or a set of possible routes. Clearly state the advantages and disadvantages of the different courses of action.

When decisions need to be taken, leaders must be seen to be taking them. Sometimes this involves painting a picture of what will happen if the changes do not happen.

Stage 2: People start to react to the change

People may at first feel concern, anger, resentment or fear. They may correctly identify real threats to their positions and may resist the change actively or passively. They may feel the need to express their feelings and concerns, and vent their anger. This stage is the 'danger zone.' If this stage is badly managed, the organization may descend into crisis or chaos. Therefore this stage needs careful planning and preparation. As someone responsible for change, you should prepare for this stage by carefully considering the impacts and objections that people may have. Make sure that you address these early with clear communication and support and by taking action to minimize and mitigate the problems that people will experience. As the reaction to change is very personal and can be emotional, it is often impossible to pre-empt everything, so make sure that you listen and watch carefully during this stage or have mechanisms to help you get information so you can respond to the unexpected.

For as long as people resist the change and remain at Stage 2, the change will be unsuccessful, at least for the people who react in this way. This is a stressful and unpleasant stage. It is much healthier to move to Stage 3 where pessimism and resistance give way to some optimism and acceptance.

It is important to realize that people's reaction to change can be extremely negative and it may even affect their health. Be careful not to simply believe that people are being stubborn; change may affect them negatively in a very real way that you not have foreseen.

Stage 3: People stop focusing on what they have lost

At this stage, people start to let go, and accept the change. They begin testing and exploring what the changes mean, and so learn the reality of what's good and not so good, and how they must adapt. This is the turning point for individuals and for the organization. You then start to feel you are on the way to making a success of the change. Individually, as people's acceptance grows, they'll need to test and explore what the change means. They will do this more easily if they are helped and supported, even if this is a simple matter of allowing enough time to adapt.

As the person managing the change, you can lay good foundations for this stage by making sure that people are well trained, and are given early opportunities to experience what the changes will bring. Be aware that this stage is vital for learning and acceptance, and that it takes time. Don't expect people to be 100 per cent productive during this time, and build in contingency time so that people can learn and explore without too much pressure.

Stage 4: People not only accept change but also start to embrace it

People rebuild their ways of working. Only when they get to this stage can the organization start to reap the benefits of change. This is where the changes start to become second nature, and people embrace the improvements to the way they work. As someone managing change, this is where you will start to see the benefits of your hard work in making the change transition as smooth as possible. Your team or organization start to become productive and efficient, and the positive effects of change become apparent.

Remember to celebrate success when appropriate! People will at the very least have been uncomfortable and everyone deserves to share the success. Also, celebration may pave the way to make things easier for future changes.

With knowledge of the Change curve, you can plan how you'll minimize the negative impact of the change and help people understand and adapt more quickly to it.

Kurt Lewin's change management model

Lewin, a physicist as well as social scientist, explained organizational change using the analogy of changing the shape of a block of ice. If you have a large cube of ice, but realize that what you want is a cone of ice, what do you do? First you must melt the ice to make it amenable to change (unfreeze). Then you must mould the icy water into the shape you want (change). Finally, you must solidify the new shape (refreeze).

By looking at change as a process with distinct stages, you can prepare yourself for what is coming and make a plan to manage the transition. To begin any successful change process, you must first start by understanding why the change must take place.

This model states that there are three stages of change. It describes how you generally have to 'break up' the current state of things in order to make improvements, using the concept of 'unfreeze–change–refreeze'.

Unfreeze

Resistance to change should be minimized. This entails the management detailing what the consequences of any change would be for all stakeholders, and also outlining what would happen if change did not take place.

> Lewin stated: 'Motivation for change must be generated before change can occur. One must be helped to re-examine many cherished assumptions about oneself and one's relations to others.'

To prepare the organization to accept that change is necessary, it is necessary to break down the existing status quo before you can build up a new way of operating. The key to this is developing a compelling message showing why the existing way of doing things cannot continue.

To prepare the organization successfully, you need to start at its core – you need to challenge the beliefs, values, attitudes and behaviours that currently define it.

This first part of the change process is usually the most difficult and stressful. When you start cutting down the 'way things are done', you put everyone and everything off balance. You may evoke strong reactions in people, and that's exactly what needs to done.

Old ideals and processes must be tossed aside so that new ones may be learned. Often, getting rid of the old processes is just as difficult as learning new ones due to the power of habits. During this part of the process you may need to provide some coaching as people are unlearning and need emotional support to break the old habits.

The transition from unfreeze to change does not happen overnight: people like to take time to embrace the new direction and participate pro-actively in the change. A related change model, the 'Change curve model' described above, focuses on the specific issue of personal transitions in a changing environment and is useful for understanding this specific aspect in more detail.

Changing

After the uncertainty created in the unfreeze stage, the change stage is where people begin to resolve their uncertainty and look for new ways to do things. People start to believe and act in ways that support the new direction.

In order to accept the change and contribute to making the change successful, people need to understand how the changes will benefit them. Not everyone will fall in line just because the change is necessary and will benefit the company. This is a common assumption and pitfall that should be avoided.

This period also requires emotional support as there may be confusion, overload and despair, but there will also be hope, discovery and excitement. This period requires coaching and possibly training as people are learning new things.

Unfortunately, some people will genuinely be harmed by change, particularly those who benefit strongly from the status quo. Others may take a long time to recognize the benefits that change brings. You need to foresee and manage these situations.

Time and communication are the two keys to success for the changes to occur. People need time to understand the changes and they also need to feel highly connected to the organization throughout the transition period. When you are managing change, this can require a great deal of time and effort, and hands-on management is usually the best approach.

When the changes are taking shape and people have embraced the new ways of working, the organization is ready to refreeze.

Refreezing

The new processes are now intellectually and emotionally accepted. What has been learned is now actually being practised on the job. It can take six to eight weeks to change habits before you can start to feel comfortable again.

The refreeze stage also needs to help people use the new changes all the time, and ensure that they are incorporated into everyday business. With a new sense of stability, employees feel confident and comfortable with the new ways of working.

The rationale for creating a new sense of stability in our ever-changing world is often questioned. Even though change is a constant in many organizations, this refreezing stage is still important. Without it, employees get caught in a transition trap where they aren't sure how things should be done, so nothing ever gets done to full capacity. In the absence of a new frozen state, it is very difficult to tackle the next change initiative effectively. How do you go about convincing people that something needs changing if you haven't allowed the most recent changes to sink in? Change will be perceived as change for change's sake, and the motivation required to implement new changes simply won't be there.

As part of the refreezing process, make sure that you celebrate the success of the change – this helps people to find closure; thank them for enduring a painful time and help them believe that future change will be successful.

Mission and vision statements are a well-structured way of helping you to communicate what the change is intended to achieve, and to motivate everyone with an inspiring, shared vision of the future. (See the suggested mission statement for professional assistants in Chapter 4 on 'Leading effective teams to success').

Summary

You have to work hard at making change progress smoothly, effectively and successfully. When you plan carefully and build the proper foundation, implementing change can be much easier, and you'll improve the chances of success. If you are too impatient, and if you expect too many results too soon, your plans for change are more likely to fail.

Understanding the different models of change, and in particular 'the change curve', which allows you to understand and know what to expect emotionally at the different stages, has helped me enormously throughout my working life. I have learned to accept change at each stage, which has helped to reduce the pain and has taught me that once you are through the change, everything always turns out for the best. This chapter will help you to help yourself and others to have a smooth and painless transition through any change. Adopt the right attitude, help and encourage others to understand the process, and realize that with hindsight all change can be extremely worthwhile. Help others look for the good in change and realize what exciting opportunities can arise for them. Keep positive and positive things will happen to you. Helping yourself, your boss and colleagues through the change process will prove your skills as a strategic business partner and you will enable the achievement of goals and objectives that are aligned with the ever evolving business strategy.

I hope you now perceive the process of change as something to be excited about. Change brings opportunities that can open up for you. Being at the forefront of change is much more empowering as it gives you a feeling of being in control, so get involved and help others.

You now have methods and tools to help you think positively about change; remember to regularly ask yourself the empowering questions. You now know how to get rid of limiting beliefs and replace them with empowering beliefs to bring you success, happiness and fulfilment.

RESOURCE 1

The global list of professional administrative associations produced by *The Executive Secretary* magazine

You can find this list which is constantly being updated at **www.executive-secretary.com**; if you wish to add your association to the website free of charge then please e-mail Lucy Brazier, editor and publisher of *The Executive Secretary* magazine at **lbrazier@executivesecretary.com**. You can also add your events free of charge.

Asia

Association of Secretaries and Administrative Professionals (ASAP)
www.asapap.org

Australia

Executive Assistant Network (EAN)
www.execassist.com.au
Australian Institute of Office Professionals (AIOP)
www.aiop.com.au

Austria

European Management Assistants (EUMA)
www.euma.org

Bahamas

IAAP Chapter
www.iaapbahamas.com

Bangladesh

Professional Secretaries' Welfare Association (PSWA)
www.pswab.org

Barbados

Barbados Association of Office Professionals (BAOP)
www.baop.org

Belgium

European Management Assistants (EUMA)
www.euma.org
Association Lie 'geoise des Secre' taires et Assistant(e)s de Direction (ALISAD)
www.alisad.be

Brazil

Sindicato das Secretárias do Estado de São Paulo (SINSESP)
www.sinsesp.com.br
FENASSEC
www.fenassec.com.br

Canada

Federation Des Secretaires Professionnelles du Quebec (FSPQ)
http://www.fspq.qc.ca/
The Social Network for Virtual Assistants
www.vanetworking.com
Association of Administrative Assistants
www.aaa.ca
adminassist.ca
www.adminassist.ca

Cape Verde

Association Professional Secretariat in Cape Verde (APSCV)
www.apscv.cv

Caribbean

Caribbean Association of Secretaries & Administrative Professionals (casap)
www.casap-online.org

Costa Rica

Federacão Interamericana de Associacõ de Secretarias (FIAS)
N/A

Cyprus

European Management Assistants (EUMA)
www.euma.org

Denmark

European Management Assistants (EUMA)
www.euma.org

Europe (All Countries)

European Management Assistants (EUMA)
www.euma.org

Finland

Sihteeriyhdistys – Sekreterarföreningen ry
www.sihteeriyhdistys.fi
European Management Assistants (EUMA)
www.euma.org

France

Cercle des Assistantes et Secrétaires (CLASS)
www.class6942.free.fr
European Management Assistants (EUMA)
www.euma.org

Germany

Bundesverband Sekretariat und Büromanagement e.V. (bSb)
www.bsb-office.de
European Management Assistants (EUMA)
www.euma.org

Greece

European Management Assistants (EUMA)
www.euma.org

Hong Kong

Hong Kong Association of Secretaries and Administrative Professionals (HKASAP)

Hungary

European Management Assistants (EUMA)
www.euma.org

Iceland

European Management Assistants (EUMA)
www.euma.org

India

Indian Association of Secretaries and Administrative Professionals (IASAP)
www.iasapindia.com

Indonesia

Ikatan Sekretaris Indonesia (ISI)
www.isi-bandung.com

Italy

AssistenteDirezione.it
www.assistentedirezione.it

ManagementAssistant.it
www.managementassistant.it
Secretary.IT Manager Assistant Network
www.secretary.it
MACSE Italia – Manager Assistant Carriera Sviluppo Evoluzione (MACSE)
www.macseitalia.it
European Management Assistants (EUMA)
www.euma.org

Jamaica

Jamaica Association of Secretaries & Administrative Professionals (JASAP)
www.jasap-online.org

Japan

Japan Office Professional Alliance (JOPA)
http://www.jopa-hq.org/public/
Japan Secretaries Association (JSA) **www.hishokyokai.or.jp/english** (JSA)
www.hishokyokai.or.jp/english

Luxembourg

European Management Assistants (EUMA)
www.euma.org

Malaysia

Malaysian Association of Professional Secretaries & Administrators (MAPSA)
www.mapsa-malaysia.com

Mozambique

Association of Secretaries of Mozambique
www.assemo.co.mz

Netherlands

Nederlandse Vereniging van Directiesecretaresses (NVD)
www.nvdsecretaresse.nl

European Management Assistants (EUMA)
www.euma.org

New Zealand

Association of Administrative Professionals New Zealand Inc (AAPNZ)
www.aapnz.org.nz

Norway

European Management Assistants (EUMA)
www.euma.org

Pakistan

Distinguished Secretaries' Society of Pakistan (DSSP)
www.dssp.org

Paraguay

Asociacion de Secretarias de Paraguay (ASP)
N/A

Philippines

Philippine Association of Secretaries and Administrative Professionals Inc
www.philsecretaries.org

Poland

European Management Assistants (EUMA)
www.euma.org

Portugal

Associacã de Secretarias Profissionais Portuguesas (ASP)
www.asp-secretarias.pt
European Management Assistants (EUMA)
www.euma.org

Singapore

Singapore Association of Administrative Professionals (SAAP)
www.saap.org.sg

Slovenia

Zveza klubov tajnic in poslovnih sekretarjev
www.zveza-tajnic.si
European Management Assistants (EUMA)
www.euma.org

South Africa

The Institute for Certified Administrative Professionals (ICAP)
www.competencyservices.co.za
Association for Office Professionals of South Africa (OPSA)
www.opsa.org.za

South Korea

Korea Association of Administrative Professionals (KAAP)
N/A

Spain

Asociacion del Secretariado Profesional de Aragon (ASPA)
www.asparagon.com
Asociación del Secretariado Profesional de Cantabria (ASECAN)
www.asecan.net
Secretariat i Empresa (SEiEM)
http://secretariatiempresa.blogspot.com
Asociación del Secretariado Profesional de Madrid. (ASPM)
www.aspm.es
European Management Assistants (EUMA)
www.euma.org

Sri Lanka

Sri Lanka Association of Administrative & Professional Secretaries (SLAAPS)
www.slaapsonline.com

St Kitts and Nevis

National Association of Secretaries and Administrative Professionals of St Kitts (N/A)
NASAP

Sweden

Chefssekreterarna Stockholm
www.cssto.se
European Management Assistants (EUMA)
www.euma.org

Switzerland

European Management Assistants (EUMA)
www.euma.org

Taiwan

The Professional Secretaries Association of the Republic of China
www.chinesesecretary.org.tw

Thailand

Women Secretaries' Association of Thailand (WSAT)
www.secretarythailand.org

Turks and Caicos

Turks & Caicos Association of Office Professionals (TCAOP)
www.tciofficeprofessionals.org

Uganda

National Association of Secretaries & Administrative Professionals (NASAP)
www.nasap-uganda.org

United Kingdom

Oxfordshire PA Club
www.ox-pa.com/home

London Chamber of Commerce & Industry

www.londonchamber.co.uk/lcc_public/home.asp

pa-assist.com

www.pa-assist.com

Global PA Network

www.globalpanetwork.com/

SORTED

www.sorted-pa.com

The PA Club

www.thepaclub.com

Society of Virtual Assistants (SVA)

www.societyofvirtualassistants.co.uk

National Association of Administrative Staff in Schools and Colleges (NAASSC)

www.voicetheunion.org

Institute of Professional Administrators (IPA)

www.inprad.org

International Association of Virtual Assistants

www.iava.org

Institute of Administrative Management (IAM)

www.instam.org

Institute of Agricultural Secretaries and Administrators (IAgSA)

www.iagsa.co.uk

Institute of Legal Secretaries (ILS)

www.institutelegalsecretaries.com

British Society of Medical Secretaries & Administrators (BSMSA)

www.bsmsa.org.uk

Association of Virtual Assistants (UKAVA)

www.ukava.co.uk

Association of Secretaries

www.uksecretaries.co.uk

Association of Medical Secretaries, Practice Managers, Administrators and Receptionists (AMSPAR)

www.amspar.com

Association of Celebrity Assistants

www.aca-uk.com

Assoc of Personal Assistants (APA)

www.paprofessional.com

European Management Assistants (EUMA)

www.euma.org

United States

www.theofficeprofessional.com
www.theofficeprofessional.com
Association for Healthcare Administrative Professionals (AHCAP)
www.ahcap.org
Virtual Association for Administrative Professionals
www.thevaap.com
Associacion de Secretarias del Uruguay (ADESU)
www.adesu.org.uy
The Virtual Assistant Chamber of Commerce
www.virtualassistantnetworking.com
The International Virtual Assistants Association (IVAA)
www.ivaa.org
National Association for Legal Secretaries
www.nals.org
Society for Design Administration (SDA)
www.sdadmin.org
National Association for Legal Assistants
www.nala.org
IAAP – International Association of Administrative Professionals
www.iaap-hq.org
Legal Secretaries International Inc
www.legalsecretaries.org
Coaches, Authors, Speakers Professional Assistants Association
www.caspaa.com
Association of Professional Office Managers (APOM)
www.apomonline.org
Assoc of Executive and Administrative Professionals (AEAP)
www.theaeap.com
American Society of Administrative Professionals
www.asaporg.com
American Association of School Administrators (AASA)
www.aasa.org

Uruguay

Associacion de Secretarias del Uruguay (ADESU)

RESOURCE 2

Example person specification

The following is generic and an accumulation of every assistant-type role to let you know what is possible although it is not exhaustive.

Job Title:	All encompassing 'assistant' and team leader The position is busy, varied and demanding so candidates should be appropriately qualified and experienced.
Reports to:	CEO.
Responsible for:	Assistant duties to the CEO and leading/ supervising a team of assistants.
General purpose of role:	To provide a confidential and efficient assistant support service to the CEO. To effectively lead a team of assistants working for various line managers.

Person specifications normally include essential and desirable qualifications, training, experience, attributes, skills and abilities and some specifications may even include how they will be measured such as by application (past experience), by being tested either psychometric or practical or via the interview questioning.

ESSENTIAL CRITERIA	DESIRABLE CRITERIA
EDUCATIONAL REQUIREMENTS	
Good level of education. (Be more specific depending on your country's qualifications.)	Secretarial/ administration qualifications/degrees/ diplomas. Business degrees/ diplomas. Management degrees/ diplomas.

ESSENTIAL CRITERIA	DESIRABLE CRITERIA
EXPERIENCE	
Previous experience in an administrative/ secretarial/office management role (depending on what role and level of job you are advertising).	Staff supervision/ management experience. Experience of working within a professional office. Member of an assistant network (outside work on own volition).
PROFESSIONAL/TECHNICAL AND OCCUPATIONAL TRAINING	
Accurate touch typing and keyboard skills – at least 60wpm with a minimum of 95% accuracy Undertake a range of word processing duties including creating letters, statistical and narrative reports, executive summaries, agendas etc – many of which will be drafted and generated on one's own initiative. Up-to-date experience of Microsoft Office applications including PowerPoint, Excel. MS Word advanced knowledge including knowing how to use track changes, insert tables of contents, use styles, mail merge, screen shots and create hyperlinks, etc. Excellent at spelling and grammar. Proficient at taking minutes of meetings, including board meetings, plus related pre-meeting with Chair. Taking dictation either on the phone or direct with shorthand or longhand with short forms or speedwriting. Audio typing. Reading, monitoring and responding to correspondence. Proofreading plus the ability to grasp and comment on the larger concepts of the business meetings and the documents you create. Familiarity with using the internet and the intranet.	Social media savvy – good understanding and ability to effectively use social networking tools (for example LinkedIn and Twitter) to promote business services and develop relationships. Marketing knowledge. Comfortable use of keyboard short cuts to save time. Evidence of own continuing professional development. Experience of using spreadsheets and formulas. Having the curiosity and willingness to keep learning and up-skilling on all office and technological programs including technology like cloud computing and digital board meeting documents. Taking part in Board meetings such as having an agenda item for administration.

ESSENTIAL CRITERIA	DESIRABLE CRITERIA
	Shorthand or speedwriting. Writing newsletters and ability to use Microsoft publisher/Visio. Ability to update websites and intranet sites and possibly be involved with their creation.

SKILLS/KNOWLEDGE/ABILITIES: Specific Responsibilities

Assistant to the CEO

Experience of liaising with senior executives of own and other organizations, with the ability to articulate and communicate to all levels. Exceptional interpersonal skills – greet, meet and deal with clients and visitors. Collating information from different sources. Coordinating printing and binding requirements. Vetting and booking appropriate restaurants and venues. Ensuring the policies, procedures, laws and regulations are followed. Excellent organizational skills/administrative skills. Coordinate and organize the diary including internal and external meetings and attendees. Understand different management and work styles and work with them; eg if you have a detailed boss then make sure you have all the information and back-up papers; if you have a 'big-picture' boss then only go into a meeting with one sheet of bullet points to discuss and a very small pile of paper, if any at all, etc. Preparing meeting papers, itineraries and maps etc. Organize travel arrangements including visas/ money/preparing a few foreign phrases/ preparing complex travel itineraries. Travel with executive when appropriate. Gatekeeper of an executive's calendar and time. Experience with organizing events, conferences and seminars, liaising and negotiating costs with venues and suppliers.	Ability to work with VIPs in a cool, calm and collected manner. Exceptional observational skills – notice what you notice. Project management. Ability to summarize. Ability to analyse information. Own a full driving licence – attend venues, meetings and possibly act as chauffeur on occasion. Able to look after budgets. Keep up to date with the latest office gadgets and industry practices – and teach others how to use them. Bilingual/multilingual. Capable of competently dealing with situations in the boss's absence. Have strengths and become an expert in areas to complement your boss's weaknesses.

ESSENTIAL CRITERIA	DESIRABLE CRITERIA
Excellent communication skills with good command of language (verbal and written) – knowing when to speak up and having the courage to do so; knowing when to keep quiet and having the common sense to do so. The ability to build rapport and relationships with all staff, but especially your boss and your team. Ability to negotiate, debate and rationalize. Always use active listening and effective questioning techniques. Understanding of business/commercial awareness gained from study, experience or both. Being strategically aware and aligning goals with the boss and the strategy, vision and mission of the company – create stretched goals. Be aware of how PESTLE affects the company (Politics, Economics, Social, Technology, Legal and the Environment). Organizing, managing and maintaining office, including establishing and reviewing filing, bringing forward reminder systems and office systems. Daily management of e-mails including using rules, colours, files etc. The filing should emulate the hard-copy filing and your colleagues should understand the filing system in case of your absence. Undertake personal work/errands as requested – possibly even organize personal events. Answer incoming calls and take/forward messages. Well-developed, well-mannered, telephone skills and etiquette – dealing with queries and routing calls appropriately. Act as a reliable anchor point; establish good staff and client relationships; excellent client-care skills. Actively seek ways to improve the efficient running of the office. Stationery ordering/management.	Being practical – being able to use and fix photocopier, coffee machine, binder, data projector, etc. Adviser and sounding board at times. Endeavour to develop the business whenever networking externally. Find ways to work smarter not harder.

ESSENTIAL CRITERIA	DESIRABLE CRITERIA

Day-to-day management of office accounts and petty cash.

Deal with expenses, billings, credit control.

Implement processes and procedures to ensure best practice and consistent approach/delivery.

Updating and maintaining client contact database.

Dealing with the press and writing press releases, ensuring bank of photos and digital photos are up to date and in the correct format for different media.

Ability to prioritize and organize workload with strong time management skills and self-motivated – ability to work to deadlines and under pressure.

Multitasking and prioritizing – or at least being able to focus on one task at a time and getting that done whilst bearing in mind what else is required next.

Ability to maintain confidentiality, be discreet and squash gossip but at the same time appropriately be the 'eyes and ears' of your boss.

Able to work in changing circumstances and adjust working practices as required.

Share knowledge with other departments to avoid 'reinventing the wheel' and to keep them informed.

Keep an up-to-date worksheet of everything you do, enabling anyone to step in and do your job in your absence.

The ability to effectively cultivate networks both internal and external for the good of yourself, your boss and your team.

Manage your 'to do' or task lists effectively, working on the important and preventing things from becoming urgent wherever possible.

Act as an ambassador for your company and represent your boss on the phone and face to face.

Be aware of and practise ergonomics regarding health and workstation.

ESSENTIAL CRITERIA	DESIRABLE CRITERIA

SKILLS/KNOWLEDGE/ABILITIES – TEAM LEADER/SUPERVISOR SPECIFIC

Able to work in a team as well as independently and able to get on with people.

The ability to practise leadership skills; eg be visionary, set an example, understand your values, strengths and weaknesses, understand your team, know how to motivate them, establish policies and procedures, establish a team charter and an effective balanced team, think strategically.

Be prepared and plan ahead; for example organize rotas.

Healthy attitude to a work–life balance.

Ability to coach, mentor and motivate team members.

Excellent conflict management skills, diplomatic and the ability to handle grievances and difficult people.

Ability to respond not simply react.

Effective delegation skills.

Able to express appreciation of team members and be nurturing.

Organizing and chairing team meetings, including setting the agenda, liaising with the minute taker before and during the meeting; keeping control of the meeting on a timely basis and eliciting everyone's involvement.

Manage a team of assistants, ensuring day-to-day workload is efficiently and effectively monitored and fulfilled.

Conducting appraisals, helping to set strategic 'SMARTER' goals and objectives.

Staff induction, including creating and updating standard operations procedures binders.

Maintain holiday and absence records, conduct 'back to work' meetings for long or regular absences where appropriate.

Recruitment – advertising, interviewing etc.

Organizing training and team-building activities.

Firm and fair – the ability to discipline.

Maintaining appropriate cover and resources during staff absence.

Help to make work fun!

Desirable:

Aware of different cultures and etiquette, including handshake and swapping business cards – advising boss where appropriate. Understand different personality types and know how to interact with them for the most effective outcomes.

ESSENTIAL CRITERIA	DESIRABLE CRITERIA

PERSONAL ATTRIBUTES/APPEARANCE

Ability to work under pressure and to deadline.
Be sensible, level-headed and use common sense in everything you do and practise emotional intelligence.
Listen to your inner 'positive coach' and get rid of your now useless 'negative gremlins' (your negative self-talk).
The ability to read body language and use your own body language to influence and persuade using subtle matching and mirroring, pacing and leading.
Be proactive as opposed to reactive wherever possible.
Accurate attention to detail.
Sociable, friendly, amiable and supportive.
Keen to be effective – doing the right things; and efficient – doing things right.
Be loyal and true to yourself and your boss/company.
Honest, trusting and trustworthy.
A positive, optimistic and cheerful approach.
Approachable and respectful.
Have an enthusiastic, flexible and adaptable approach to work.
Outgoing and sociable personality with a sense of humour.
Resilient and assertive.
Smart professional appearance, projecting a professional image.
Achieving and maintaining a positive can do/will do attitude and want to constantly expand knowledge and be the best you can be.
Able to use own initiative, practical, thinking on your feet and responding to urgent situations.
Be calm and confident, self-assured and able to deal with pressure and to the extent it does not turn into stress.
Willing to learn and willing to volunteer for projects.
Enthusiastic, determined, diligent and tenacious.
Able to make well-informed decisions.

Tolerant and forgiving.
Act as a confidant.
Have a collaborative outlook in order to get work done.
Have a passion for the work they do.
Open-minded with a willingness to try new things.
Willing to get out of their comfort zone to learn and 'stretch' themselves.
Be someone who makes things happen.

ESSENTIAL CRITERIA	DESIRABLE CRITERIA
Punctual, dependable and reliable. Empathetic, thoughtful, sensitive and tactful – being aware of your surroundings, colleagues, office politics etc. Research and preparing quality research documents. Able to identify and foresee problems, analyse the relevant facts and information and suggest effective solutions. Able to accept responsibility, demonstrating flexibility and pride in delivering work of the highest quality. Creative and resourceful. Exemplary values, courteous, patient, polite and well mannered.	

ADDITIONAL RESPONSIBILITIES

Any other duties as requested.

RESOURCE 3

Example questions for recruiting

(Reproduced with the kind permission of Adele Woodward.)

1 Please give me an example of when you have had to manage a project/piece of work, over a period of time, to meet specific requirements.

2 Please give an example of when you've had to deal with two conflicting priorities/client matters.

3 Please give me an example of when you have developed a relationship with a member of a team/department outside your own (within your organization).

4 What are the set standards/best practices that apply in your current job?

5 Please give me an example of a new skill or specialist knowledge that you have obtained.

6 Please give me an example of two situations in which you have had to communicate in very different ways.

7 Please give me an example of when you have had to alter your communication style to ensure others understood/accepted what you were trying to convey.

8 How do you go about setting standards for/measuring the quality of your work?

9 How do you go about ensuring you fully understand your (internal or external) client's business and operating environment?

10 Please give me an example of when you have worked with a colleague who had a different working style from you. How did you handle it?

11 Tell me about a problem that a colleague has brought to you recently.

12 Can you give me an example of when your manager was absent and you were forced to make a decision? What did you take into consideration? What was the effect of your decision?

13 Tell me how you prioritize your day.

14 Give me an example of how you have responded to a colleague who seemed overworked or stressed.

15 What IT packages do you use on a day-to-day basis?

16 Can you give me an example of when you have used PowerPoint to enhance a presentation. What was the length of the presentation? Were you required to use Advanced PowerPoint features?

17 Have you used an in-house finance package before? What did you understand about its purposes?

18 Can you give me an example of when you have had to use Excel as part of your job? Did it require the use of complex formulae?

19 What systems do you have in place to enable other people to pick up your work in your absence?

20 Tell me about a time when attention to detail was critical to the success of a task. How did you achieve this?

21 Give an example of where you have had to organize the diary or commitments of other people.

22 What do you do when your time schedule is upset by unforeseen circumstances? Please give examples.

23 Tell me about what you did the last time you had a personal backlog at work?

24 How do you keep abreast of developments in your organization?

25 Tell me about a time when you have had to organize the travel arrangements, accommodation and/or conferences for others.

26 Have you had to arrange events with budget constraints?
What did you do and how?

27 Give me an example of a time when you had to adapt to a changing environment. How did you do this?

28 How do you think external factors affect your team?

29 Give me an example of when you have worked as part of a team to reach a common goal.

30 What is the best example of teamworking you have been involved in? Why? What was your contribution to the team?

31 Tell me about your most successful working relationship. What did you do to make this successful? Have you ever had to work with

someone who was not good at his/her job or was difficult?
What did you do about it?

32 Give an example of a time when you have had to encourage others to contribute to the effectiveness of the team.

33 Can you tell me about a time when you had to support another team member?

34 Have you had to manage the performance of others in the workplace? How did you accomplish this?

35 How have you actively developed your skills in your previous roles?

36 Give an example of when you delivered something beyond what was required.

37 What achievement are you most proud of and why?

38 How have you updated your skills since leaving college/school?

39 Tell me about a time when you have had to encourage a colleague.

40 How do you adapt to different personalities?

41 Give me an example of how you dealt with a confrontational situation.

42 How do you think your work colleagues view you?

43 What sort of correspondence do you draft yourself and what checks are made on it before sending it out?

44 Tell me of a time when you suggested something which was not initially accepted. Did you manage to change other people's minds, and if so how?

45 Can you give me an example of when you have had to communicate with people on different levels?

46 What is the most complex problem you have had to deal with in the workplace? How did you approach it? What was the outcome? What did you learn from this?

47 What sort of decisions do you take in your job at present? Which ones do you consult your manager on?

48 What were the steps you took in deciding to choose your career/last job?

49 Was there a time when you identified a potential problem before it became an issue?

50 Can you tell me about a time when you had to deal with a complex problem and what range of solutions did you identify?

51 What people or methods do you use when solving problems?

52 How do you find working to deadlines?

53 Tell me about your most challenging deadline.

54 Give me an example of when you had to deal with conflicting priorities.

55 Can you tell me about a time when an increase at work required you to seek support from a colleague? Who did you go to, and how did you approach the situation?

56 Can you give me an example of when you have had to anticipate a need or deadline and what you did to ensure it was met?

57 When have you gone out of your way to provide a good service?

58 How do you promote good working relationships in the office?

59 How do you gauge client satisfaction in your role?

60 How do you balance the difference between important and urgent tasks?

61 Can you tell me about a time when attention to detail was critical to a piece of work?

62 Can you tell me about a time when you have faced an opportunity to enhance the service to the client?

63 How do you build and maintain relationships with clients?

64 In your previous/current role, describe a situation where you have been faced with a problem and had to make a quick decision.

65 Can you give an example recently when you have had to work with difficult or challenging people?

66 What do you feel your strengths are and why?

67 In your previous/current role can you describe a time where you have had to organize a number of different tasks all in a short space of time? (How was this prioritized?).

68 Can you give me an example of where you have helped out another team or department?

69 Who are the main competitors/rivals to the company you most recently worked for?

70 Tell me about a time when something didn't quite work out for you or went wrong in some way. How did you feel and how did you handle it?

71 Tell me about a weakness you have, what is it and what are you doing about it?

72 Give examples of what you have done for your own self-development. Have you arranged anything for your own self-development out of work?

73 Do you belong to any assistant networks; if so how involved are you?

RESOURCE 4

Coaching questions

What is it that you want. What would be your ideal outcome?
Feel; Hear, See what it is you want in your mind's eye

Identifying options: *So now you know what you want, answer these questions*

1 What specifically have you done so far? What worked and what didn't?

2 What do you have already (eg skills and resources) that could move you forwards?

3 What research could you do to help you find the first (or next) step?

4 What do you need to do before you do anything else?

5 Who else could you ask for help in achieving your goal?

6 If you were at your best, what would you do right now?

7 What would you do if you were an expert in (the area of your goal/ problem)?

8 What would you advise your best friend to do if they were in your situation?

9 What would your best friend advise you to do?

10 What would (someone who inspires you) do in your situation?

11 If you had a choice what would you do?

12 What if you had as much time as you needed?

13 What if money were not an issue?

14 Imagine you're fully confident in your abilities; what could you do?

15 Imagine you're fully confident that others will support you. Now what could you do?

16 What other angles and options have you not thought of yet?

17 What is an impossible option?

18 What is the decision you have been avoiding?

19 If you (secretly) knew the answer to getting unstuck, what would that be?

Limiting beliefs: To challenge unrealistic or exaggerated attitudes and beliefs and to help you explore alternative perspectives

1 Where does the reaction/belief come from?

2 In what way may you be sabotaging yourself?

3 How do you know that is a correct interpretation?

4 How is that belief helping?

5 What could be a different interpretation?

6 How might ... see the situation?

7 What is stopping you?

8 What pressures do you put on yourself?

9 How could you view it differently?

Under-used resources and possibilities: To challenge you to acknowledge your strengths and to surface underused resources and explore possibilities for achieving your goals

1 What are your unused skills/resources?

2 What are your current strengths? What else? What else? What else?

3 What opportunities do you let go by?

4 What ambitions remain unfulfilled?

5 What could you be doing that you are not doing?

6 What are you failing to accomplish – what opportunities do you need to be developing?

7 What role models could you be emulating?

8 What could this opportunity look like if you developed it?

9 What are the possibilities for a better future?

10 What are some wild possibilities for making your life better?

11 If money/time/resources were no obstacle, what options might you choose?

Blockers and enablers: *To establish what you perceive will help or hinder the achievement of goals*

1 Where does the reaction/belief come from?
2 What is getting in the way?
3 What is stopping you?
4 What are the main barriers?
5 What is going well that you can build on?
6 What are the pressures on you now?
7 What are your fears about making change?
8 What do you find comfortable now that may be holding you back?
9 What are the benefits to you of making this change?
10 What are your concerns if you don't do anything?

Motivation: *To define the gap between the current and preferred situation and to clarify goals*

1 What would this problem look like if you were managing it better?
2 What would make this time well spent for you?
3 Tell me how you see things at the moment.
4 What needs to be resolved?
5 What do you really want?
6 What would you like to achieve today?
7 What is troubling you?
8 How would you like things to look a year from now?
9 How would you like things to be different?
10 What are your concerns?

Implementation: *To give realistic encouragement and feedback and help with resources as necessary*

1 What worked well for you?
2 What didn't work well for you?
3 What's not gone according to plan?

4 What has been unexpected?

5 What might you consider doing differently next time?

Review: progress and learning

1 How can we use the remaining time most effectively?

2 What do we need to refocus on?

3 What are you prepared to do differently?

4 Are we dealing with the key areas?

5 How are you doing?

6 What new insights have you gained?

7 What area do you feel would be most beneficial to address now?

8 What have you learned from the process?

9 How will I know you've completed your action/s?

Commitment: Do something – explore strategies for accomplishing goals, choose the best fit strategy and formulate an action plan

When specifically will you do your action/s? Include the day and time.

On a scale of 1 to 10, how likely are you to complete each action? If it's below an 8, then ask what is stopping you from completing the action – and make this your first action.

1 How do you normally sabotage yourself – and what will you do differently this time?

2 How will I know you've completed your action/s?

3 Who will you tell about your actions (to support you in completing them)?

4 What specifically will you ask your supporters to do for you?

5 Tell me how you'll feel once you have completed your actions.

6 How will you reward yourself when you complete your actions?

Taking action: Look at the list of ideas and options you now have

1 What are some of the things you might do?

2 How might you minimize obstacles?

3 How many different ways are there to accomplish what you want?

4 What would be the smallest or easiest first step for you?

5 Which options or actions grab you?

6 How could you make the tasks/actions more enjoyable or fun?

7 What might be some unintended consequences of these actions?

8 What data will you need to collect as feedback as you move forward?

9 Who else could help you in completing your actions?

10 What's one action you could take in the next 10 minutes?

11 What are three actions you could take that would make sense this week?

12 Where do you go from here?

13 On a scale of 1–10, what is your level of commitment to your plan?

14 What's next – what steps are involved?

RESOURCE 5

Wheel of life

Write down a brief description for each category as if you were feeling total satisfaction and achievement. Imagine what it would look like, feel like and what you would hear if each category was marked with a 10!

Category	Description of total satisfaction
Money	
Hobbies	
Personal Development	
Health	

RESOURCE 6

Blank 'Wheel of life' – to use creatively

TITLE: _____

Examples: 'Competency Wheel of life'; 'Action-planning Wheel of life'; 'Goal-setting Wheel of life'

NAME: _____   DATE: _____

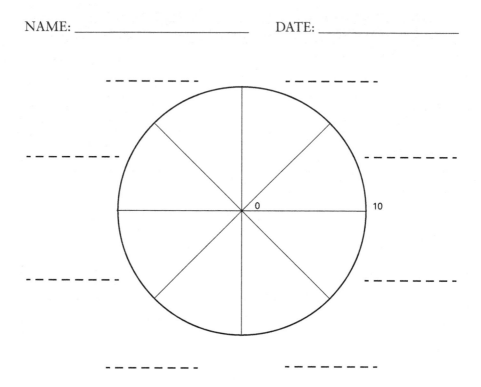

INSTRUCTIONS:

Please change, split and name the sections so that they are meaningful to you.
The centre of the wheel is 0 and the outer edge is 10.
Rank your level of satisfaction or frustration (depending on how you use the wheel) for each area out of 10 by drawing a line across the section that represents your number (see example)
This now represents your
" _ _ _ _ _ _ _ _ _ _ _ _ _ _ _ _ _ _ "
'Wheel of Life'

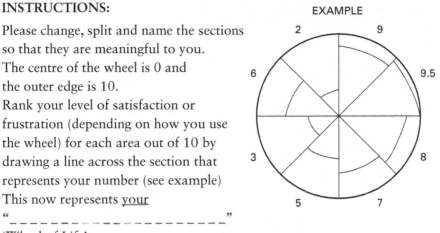

EXAMPLE

E-mail: sue@suefrance.com
I would love to hear your innovative ideas on how you use this form
Sue France Training
www.suefrance.com

RESOURCE 7

Preparation form for all negotiations

Think of your own position as well as the other person/party's position

Brief description of the negotiation:		
	Mine/ours	**Theirs**
The ideal and best outcome: 'Aspire to'		
Realistic and satisfactory outcome: 'Content with'		
Acceptable minimum bottom line/fallback position: 'Live with'		
The essentials required (what we need/must have)		
The desirables required (what we want/would like to have)		

Possible concessions		
Possible trade off		
Best alternative to a negotiated agreement (BATNA)		
Consequences of winning or losing		
Preferred negotiation style		
Negotiation style to be used in this negotiation		
Power: Who has what power in the relationship? Who controls resources? Who stands to lose the most if agreement isn't reached? What power does the other person have to deliver what you hope for?		
Opening statement:		

Type of relationship I would like to have when the negotiation is over:

Possible solutions based on all of the considerations:

Expected outcome:

INDEX

NB page numbers in *italic* indicate figures or tables

CPSIA information can be obtained
at www.ICGtesting.com
Printed in the USA
BVOW06s0958060117

472833BV00007B/19/P